KU-431-994

DO I COME HERE OFTEN?

Black Coffee Blues Pt 2

Henry Rollins

First published in Great Britain in 2005 by
Virgin Books Ltd
Thames Wharf Studios
Rainville Road
London W6 9HA

Published in USA 1996 by 2.13.61 Publications

Copyright © Henry Rollins 1996

This book is sold subject to the condition that it shall not, by way of
trade or otherwise, be lent, resold, hired out or otherwise circulated
without the publisher's prior written consent in any form of binding
or cover other than that in which it is published and without a similar
condition including this condition being imposed upon the
subsequent purchaser.

A catalogue record for this book is available from the British Library.

ISBN 978 0 7535 1040 7

Typeset by TW Typesetting, Plymouth, Devon
Printed and bound in Great Britain by
CPI Antony Rowe, Chippenham, Wiltshire

DO I COME HERE OFTEN?

CONTENTS

ACKNOWLEDGMENTS
Thanks: Selby, Bajema, Vega, Mitch Bury
of Adams Mass.

JOE COLE 4.10.61–12.19.91

HAPPY BIRTHDAY

2.13.87 12:10 a.m. Amtrak en route to Chicago IL Two girls walk by. 'Where do you think Henry's going?' I should dress up in a Cyndi Lauper suit. I'm going to Madison, WI for a show. The closest Amtrak can get me is Chicago. No sweat. I just turned 26 on this train. No more of that 'Quarter Century Man' shit for me anymore, I'm on my way to thirty.

Just spent three days in DC. Finished up all the East Coast shows: New York, Boston, Providence, New Haven, Trenton, New Brunswick, DC. Sure was great to see Ian. It's hard to think of that boy turning twenty-five. I really can't see it happening. Not that I think he's going to die before he gets there or anything, but I thought that maybe he would magically escape aging. There is something about him that transcends age. *Eternal* is such a heavy, clumsy word. I don't want to use it. He's like a season. I know he'll be around. No plane crash will get that guy. Still, it makes me think. What a trip. Ian MacKaye, twenty-five. No way.

The thing I got from this visit is that now it's just like another town. I don't even remember the names of the streets. Most of the people I know have moved away. I don't know most of the people that hang out. I think that the less people I know, the better. I'm not going to visit there anymore, only to play. I don't need any time among friends. When I open my mouth, I waste my time when I do those things. I lie to myself. There's no use in that. When I'm in the room with them, I feel uneasy, they feel uneasy. It's a lie, it doesn't work. It doesn't have to work. People games tangle me up. Get me caught in games with myself.

The whole car of this train is alive with noise. All of the people behind me are drunk. I can't see why they put alcohol on trains. The air is thick with the smell of booze and bad food.

A drunk guy in front of me is telling us all about how all these people he knows thinks he's a genius and he says, 'Hah! To me, it's nothing!'

The old folks across the aisle talk about boring shit, their kids, *The Bill Cosby Show* and food, that's it. The man with the cowboy hat should be executed. He's walking up and down the aisle, yelling,

'Does anyone want a beer?'

Some guy yells, 'Yeah, I'll take one! He's got a white hat on, he must be a good guy!'

The man behind me croaks, 'Yeah! Bring 'em down!'

Now I hear some people up ahead.

'Did you see that guy with the short hair?'

The citizens are a trip. Thank goodness for Bruce Springsteen to keep all these people in line. Hey! Go to work, be the person you hate, suck your employer's ass, come home and drink. It's all right, Bruce Springsteen wrote a song about you. If you didn't get in line and work all day and hate your own guts then the Boss wouldn't have anything to write about and he'd go out of business. The citizen and the Boss walk hand-in-hand into the darkness. I don't mind his music though. In a situation like this, I see where he's coming from.

Four more shows on this trip. Then back to LA for four weeks then out to Trenton for band practice and tour.

Looking forward to getting back out here. California is a kicked back joke.

2.13.88 1:07 a.m. Chicago IL I am twenty-seven years old. Did the show here tonight. Had a real cool time. Went for an hour and a half – it felt like ten minutes.

Stayed up late last night. Tried to get the train at 7:00 a.m. but it was sold out. Had to fly. The airplane was overbooked so they put me in first class. It was cool. It was strange to look back and see all these sorry looking folks in coach. I couldn't help it. I kept looking back at them and watched them watching me. Got off the plane, did two interviews on the phone at the airport. Took a cab to this neighborhood where I always go to get books. Found *Proud Beggars* by Albert Cossery. Went from there to the club, did two interviews. Took ten minutes to get ready, went out and hit it. Did an interview after everybody cleared out. It was strange. All these people wanted to talk to me. I'm signing all these books and then they had to leave and they freaked. They started shoving all this stuff in front of me to sign and started grabbing me. A trip.

So tired from the last few days that I can't even think straight enough to write. The interviews are hard to do. I don't know how much more I can keep this up. I have to get some sleep. Every day has been a brain fry.

I can feel the beast crawling into my bones. My friend is back. There's that hard skin I lose when I'm back there. It's coming back. That's when I'm on – when the beast is running through my blood. I can feel it and it's so good. I knew there was something missing and now it's back. The longer I'm out, the better it gets. It's so easy to forget. When I'm back there, it destroys parts of me, makes me dull. It takes a while for the hard shine to come back. What I really need is the music. This spoken thing is good but I need the pain that the music inflicts on my body. That's when I'm at my best. Hard to explain to other people. I have to stay away from women. The longer I go without sex, the better. When I'm with a woman, I get weak. No one is close to me and when I'm in close contact with a woman, I try to get out of myself. I lie to myself and that's bullshit. For me to do what I need to do, I can be close to no one.

I have been frustrated the last few weeks because I haven't had enough stimuli. I keep wanting to be back in Europe in the fourth month of the tour, meaner than shit. I haven't been tested since December. I need it bad. I don't think I should ever come off the road. If I do, I should go to a place where I don't know anyone. Association weakens me, waters me down. I will not let anyone pull me off the trail. I must re-read the iron reminders that I wrote a few months ago. They are the truth. The part about how the work comes before anything and anyone, even me. The mission is the only thing that matters. Sex, relationships come second place, third place, last place. The work is all there is.

I remember a while ago. I was with this girl, I told her that the work comes before anything. She got offended. Hey fuck that shit. Females play a smaller part in my life than they used to. As soon as they get in the way of the work then it makes me not like them. They don't know me. No one knows me. The work knows me. The road knows me. The beast knows me. Conflict knows me. Women make all that stuff taste cheap. I was with this girl recently. When I hit the road, I missed her for about a day and now I don't think of her at all. Time to fall out. Tomorrow is Madison, Wisconsin. Another day. Bring them all on. Let them destroy me, let them try. I welcome the hard things.

2:40 p.m. Madison WI Got here a couple of hours ago. Been outside a long time. Now I'm inside Victor's coffee store listening to two men discuss why drinking coffee makes them feel guilty. I'm so cold that I can hardly hold the pen. I got a pot of coffee – that will allow me to stay here long enough to thaw out. Have to do an interview soon. It's too cold to go back out there too soon.

Looking at all the brightly dressed college kids walking down the street makes me glad that I chose not to go that route. Hearing the shit they talk about is beyond belief. I can't understand how people of that age can be into such mindless bullshit.

I was thinking about how today is my birthday. I came to this: Who gives a fuck? It's just another day. I was in this town a year ago doing a talking show. Tomorrow is Milwaukee then on to Boston for the better part of a week. Will be good to move on to another part of the country. I have been out almost two weeks, I can't even tell. I have to look at my interview list to find out what day it is. I like doing the shows night after night without nights off. They get better and better when I do a lot of shows straight. Momentum is important. I find that it helps me to be able to free associate and work openly while on stage.

While on the street, people pass me, about once a block I hear my name being mentioned. 'That's Henry Rollins,' 'Where,' 'There,' 'Wow,' and so on. At this point I thought I would be used to it. I'm not, but it doesn't bug me like it used to. I have learned that there is a space in my head where I can go where no one can get to me. Often when I'm on the street, that's where I am. I have learned to find open fields in the space of the seat on a bus.

Now the coffee place is full of people and they're knocking into me with their shopping bags. I put the headphones on and I'm out of there. Every once in a while I look up and I see all these people looking at me like they want to sit down. Hey fuck them. All the guys look like Robin Williams. Those Docksiders kill me. Maybe they should have to stand. Maybe they should freeze to death.

Walking around here makes me sick. I don't like college towns. The streets are full of people wearing the same clothes. It's like being stuck in a wine cooler commercial and not being able to find the exit door.

2.23.89 2:56 a.m. Arlington VA Have been unable to write for a long time. Hand has been fucked up. The story is long and boring. Haven't written in weeks. Just thinking about it fucks me up. Fucks me up to the point where I don't feel like writing anymore right now.

3:02 p.m.: Like I said it's a long fucked up story. I'll make it short. A few weeks ago we were in Geelong, Australia playing. We're doing the show – all is well. This guy is standing in front of me, spitting mouthfuls of beer in my face. After a few mouthfuls, I got fed up and punched him. My fist hit his mouth. He fell out. His friends dragged him away. Moments later he came back up to the front. His face was bloody. He pulled his upper lip up and his front teeth were gone. I felt bad about it. Not because I hit the guy but because I knew that the police would be there soon to arrest me. I looked at my hand and there was a hole over the knuckle, deep enough to where I could see my tendon working. I showed it to our drummer and he was not at all interested.

A few moments later something hits the stage. Our guitar player picks it up. It's the guy's teeth – bridgework. Not much to me, another drunk asshole in my face who got destroyed, but I held onto them all the same. I figured they would be a good souvenir.

The next day the band had a day off and I had a talking show and interviews. My hand had started to swell and the pain was getting harder to take by the hour. The next day we left for the airport. My hand had turned purple and looked like it was going to explode.

The plane ride was hellish. The pain was enough that I was passing out and coming to all the way there. I was running a fever as well.

I got to LA about fourteen hours later and had to exchange the Australian money and handle all this business while in excruciating pain.

I got back to my place and, of course, the first thing I do is call up a girl I know and arrange a date for that night. Brainless.

The next day I checked into a hospital after my friend who used to be a nurse saw my hand and threw me in her car and sped me to the hospital. I figured they would give me some penicillin and that would be it. How wrong can a man be? Wrong as I was.

I went into the emergency room and the lady took one look at my hand and all of a sudden there was a doctor in my face. He said that I should fill out the forms immediately so that he could start operating as soon as possible. I told him that there wasn't going to be any operation. He said that I could leave and come back tomorrow when they would amputate my hand, or I could get started today and they would try to save what was left of my finger. This sobered me up and I filled out the form.

Minutes later I'm on my back in one of those nightgown things, there's an i.v. thing attached to my hand and I'm heading towards surgery.

At some point I woke up and the doctor came in to see how I was. He pulled off the bandage and there was this big hole in my hand. He said they were going to leave it open so it could drain. Then he gave me a shot of Demerol and I hallucinated for a while and passed out.

To make a long story short, I was in the hospital for six and a half days. On my birthday, I came to the conclusion that I had enough. I took the i.v. out of my hand and got dressed. When the doctor came in, I told him to congratulate me because today was the day that I was going home. He said that I wasn't going home for four more days. I just smiled and told him that I was leaving in a few minutes and he better make a prescription for whatever it was that I needed. He got the point and wrote a sheet for something. I got out of there and hit the road the next day. I had shows to do. I spent my 28th birthday sweating it out in a hospital bed. How weak.

I learned a good lesson this time. No asshole is worth this much trouble.

2.13.90 11:50 p.m. San Francisco CA I'm in Don and Jane's apartment. It's cool to see Don, but the situation with Don and Jane is fucked up. She takes every opportunity to rip on him. He takes it without complaining. She says the meanest things to him in front of other people. Don tries to be cool and deal with it but you can tell it hurts him a lot. They had some people over for my birthday and it was ok, I guess. I appreciate the thought but it's not my kind of thing.

It was hard to take with a room full of Jane's friends, listening to her lay into Don and make fun of him in front of all of them and their daughter. I will never get married as long as I live. I am around them and it reminds me of when I was growing up and all the acrimony between my mother and father. I watched them battle it out and had to take it from their new wives and boyfriends. There's nothing I can see that is good about marriage. I might be lonely a lot of the time but at least I have the option to get up and go when I want to. I'll hold onto that one as long as I'm breathing.

Now I'm in their spare room trying not to make too much noise for fear of unleashing the wrath of the beast known as Jane.

I have a show in town tomorrow. I am twenty-nine years old. I am lonely and poor and don't know how I am going to keep my band together and keep the books coming out. Sometimes it's all I can do to not break into pieces. I am wracked with anxiety so bad sometimes that I am unable to sleep. All I can do is get madder and madder and wait for the morning to come so I can get to work and try to keep it all going.

Luckily I am hard as hell and can take this bullshit month after month. Sometimes I feel so tired. I can't seem to get enough sleep. Never seems to help anyway.

2.13.91 12:34 a.m. Trenton NJ I am thirty years old. I am in the basement of Sim's mom's house. Have not checked in for a while. Too burned out to do so. It's not as if there's been a lot happening.

Things that happened: We did a demo yesterday. I don't know how many songs. I did the vocal overdubs today. Went fast, just hearing the basic tracks unmixed, it already sounds good to me.

I did the show in Big Bear, California the other day. I will write more about that soon when I feel more like writing.

The woman that I have been writing about for months, the woman that filled my thoughts with light, she dumped me for some guy. What a putdown. It's hard to take it. I liked her too much I guess. It occurred to me the last time I was with her that if it was this good to be with her, being without her would be bad. I feel better now, feeling better with every day that passes. A few days ago, like last Sunday, I was in the pits. I don't remember crawling like that.

She went away to Europe for a month. All the time she was gone, I thought of her constantly. Sometimes thinking of her was the only thing holding me together. All this time away, she never called, never wrote, nothing. I faxed her three times. It was the only number that she gave me. She finally got back, a few days late. I had been calling her place everyday leaving messages. She's back and I was all excited to talk to her but she was all cool and detached. I knew that something was up. She told me that she had started going out with this guy that she was working with and she didn't know which one she wanted, and that she was very confused. I talked to her a few more times trying to tell her how I felt. I knew that she was going to dump me and I was desperate and pathetic. All the time this was going down, I had to do the date in Big Bear. I had to be with all these people, shake hands and all that shit. I was dying inside the whole time. She said she would call me on Sunday morning. I finally got in touch with her in the evening and I asked her what her deal was. She still gave me the bullshit. I asked her if she had been with him since she had gotten back. She said yes. I told her that she had obviously made up her mind. It went on like that for a while, all bullshit. Finally we hung up. I called her later, but all I got was the answering machine. She broke me pretty good. It hurts to think of her with that guy. I know that he will fuck her up like he fucked up the last woman he was with. I will never understand. If someone had told me that it was going to end like this I would have told them that they were crazy. All the time that we were together, I thought we were close, it was great. I thought I meant more to her. I was wrong. I definitely learned a lesson this time. I know that I can be broken. I am not as tough as I thought. I see it now. At this point, it's the only thing good that came out of all of this. I know myself better now and know what I have to do. It always comes back to me. There's really nothing else for me but the road and the work. They are always there for me.

It was a mistake to get that interested in a woman. I learned something and I should not forget it. What happened is what should have happened – what would've happened eventually. The only thing that has not abandoned me is the road and the life. It is the one constant in my life. Movement. Constant movement and hard travel. Living out of my backpacks and sleeping on floors. I was not meant to come out of the storm.

Should go to sleep now. I have to go into the city tomorrow to meet with a guy from a record company. Yet another meeting. Over a year of meetings and the band still has no label.

2.13.92 3:20 p.m. Hamburg Germany Tonight will be the second night here. The Ahoy. I don't think I've ever played this venue besides last night. Usually we play at the Markthalle. I am thirty-one years old today. Not really an age to think about. I used to think that my birthday was an interesting date and now I don't care. I know I'll be remembering 12.19.91 forever though. It will be strange when Joe has been dead for a year.

All I can do is keep playing my guts out every night and try to sleep it off. I feel violent all the time these days. I don't particularly hate anyone, but I feel like I don't care about anything. I play the music every night merely to punish it and punish myself.

2.13.93 11:23 p.m. Leicester UK Don Bajema arrived here alright and the books got in as well. We did a show here tonight. Don was good but he didn't think so. He started a little cold but other than that it was a good show for him. I'm sure tomorrow night he'll really let it rip. I felt good about my set. People were great as they have been for pretty much the entire trip.

Last night I did a show called *The Word*. I had to sit around for a few hours before I could go sit on a couch and have my time wasted by a bunch of TV people. The only good things about it were hanging out with the guys in Living Colour and ripping on Bob Geldof when I saw him walking down the halls. His girlfriend, Paula Yates, was on the show with me. She's a typical groupie made good, a total waste of daily feeding and maintenance. The whole thing was a bore until the band that was playing started giving the host shit and he wasn't ready for it and it blew his mind. The record company made it seem like my appearance on this show was the biggest deal in the world, but you know how they are.

I was just in Holland and Belgium and the shows were good but the press got to me. I had to talk to the hag at *Kerrang!* about why I don't like two of her writers. These guys talk shit and I call them on it. They go whining to her about it and she makes it out like the world is on fire. These people are so full of their own shit that they can't see anything. None of their shit matters to me. I don't care about being in their magazine and I don't want to know about all the stupid fucking bands that they put in it. The magazine didn't like me before she got there but because she wants to fuck me, I get in the mag. These people should get a life.

I had to waste my editing time talking to this common slag. When that was over, I went right into five interviews and then to the gig. Kicked it for two hours. Felt good. All the shows have been going well. There's nothing much to write about because I don't give a fuck about writing down the stupid common details of my little life anymore. It's all the same shit all the time anyway, so fuck it. These reporters can all go get fucked. So weak – they make me weak too with their bullshit. I must not let them get to me and drag me down. You should have seen that little swine lady with her tape recorder while we were driving. A disgusting business I'm in. I get everything I deserve and deserve everything I get. I am thirty-two years old.

2.13.94 1:24 a.m. Sapporo Japan I'm thirty-three. Show was pretty good tonight. I got a workout at a mediocre gym. Hope to find better gyms down the road. We fly in the morning to Fukuoka which is way south of here. Hope there's a lot less snow. I'm too tired to write anymore.

11:29 p.m. Fukuoka Japan: Took all day to get here. The flight was delayed about three hours because of all the snow. Pretty boring. Too bad we couldn't get a gig for tonight. It was good to get away from all that snow.

Went to Tower here and found a few things. Went out and ate and then the rest of them tried to get me to go to a karaoke bar and waste time. I was out of there. Now I'm here and it's boring. Looks like I'll get an early night and that's it. I'm ready to leave. I don't think I'm in the right mood for this stuff anymore. Maybe it's just something that will pass. I'm just going to keep to myself for the rest of the trip. I don't relate to the rest of them and I feel better when I'm on my own. I wish things didn't affect me so much. It seems that I get fucked up too much over things. I don't know what to do to get better.

2.13.95 1:18 a.m. LA CA I'm thirty-four. Ian called me tonight. It was good to talk to him. He's the same as always – working hard and making music. He's one of the only people I know who isn't fucked up somehow. He does his thing and doesn't mess with anyone. He is a big influence on me. I wish I was more like him in a lot of ways. He has a good grip on things.

I am usually depressed on my birthday. I don't feel like working tomorrow. I have nothing else to do but that. It's late, but not that late. I guess I should try to get to sleep early so I won't be a wreck in the morning.

I went through the other journals to see where I was this time last year. Last year, it was Japan. I was in a hotel room

– bored, hungry and jet-lagging. The year before, I was in England. I think the only way to travel and still be able to have some fun would be to do it solo. If I could bring myself to do speaking dates again, that would be the way to go. I worry that I will never be able to do any of those shows again. I want to, but I am having trouble with people. Too bad. If I could go out and do a few weeks of shows, it would be good for things around here. There's never enough money around here. So many things I want to do but it's always money that gets in the way.

It's strange being in my apartment all these days in a row. I have not been in one place this long since 1983. It's strange having slept on the same mattress for three months. I don't want to get soft. I don't want to lose my edge. It's all I have.

2.13.96 8:30 a.m. Albuquerque NM At the airport on the way to Seattle for tonight's show. Last night was pretty good. It went a little long though – three hours and forty minutes. No one left and people seemed to dig it. I have to talk less at these shows though.

Today, I am thirty-five years old. It doesn't matter to me what my age is. Sure does go by quickly. Tonight I am going to record the show and hope it comes out as a good one so I can put it out as a live record. Been a while since I did one of those.

I like this town but it's going to be good to get on to Seattle. Something about this part of America is depressing. All the space, I think. Last night's promoter boy dropped us off at the airport this morning. He was a bit of a whiner. Rick, the road manager, said it took multiple phone calls to get him to wake up.

Last year on my birthday, I was in LA. Usually Ian calls me. The shows have been good but they make me kind of dull on the writing front. I give them all I have at night and when it comes time to have some other thoughts, there is no energy to put them across.

I wonder if I act like a thirty-five year old. I think I was born when my father was this age. I don't think I will ever be the family type. I think it will be a failure to be in a band on tour when I am forty. I think it is time to start thinking of what the next move will be. When I hear the music that bands are making these days, it tells me it's time to get out. It's over for people like me. A weaker, less interesting music is what people want to hear. I still like playing and everything. I just don't think I want to be around to have to listen to it and somehow be a part of it. Because you do become part of it whether you want to or not.

3:33 p.m. Seattle WA: At the usual hotel, the Edgewater. I was given free dessert at the hotel restaurant and people have been sending in gift certificates to local record stores here and in NY as presents. It's all very nice. People are very cool to me.

I am looking forward to doing this show tonight. I feel like I am on a roll. Not many left on this one. I'll be back in NY by the end of the week. The next few days will be a bit of a grind with all the drives. The day off is traveling all day to get to Memphis.

DAVID LEE ROTH

I spent the 70s locked in the prison that is school. For some, school can be a wonderful learning experience. It was for me. I learned that I truly hated it. The way I got through the ordeal was with the power of music. I lived for my records. The bands that I was into came to my rescue. The effect that a good piece of music has upon me is beyond words. I think that John Coltrane's music, if used correctly, could stop war and cure cancer.

When Ted Nugent would come roaring into town, I was there. Ted was the man – a real Rock and Roll Animal. I can remember being on my feet with barely any room to move because of all the seats and people, hearing him do 'Free For All'. All I wanted to do was wreck shit.

One night, me and my pal Ian MacKaye ventured out to see our main man 'The Nuge'. We saw an amazing thing happen. The opening band was up there playing and they weren't acting like any opening band. If you didn't know any better, you would think that this band *was* the band that you were there to see. The guitar player had a thing that I had never heard anywhere. It was absolutely savage. And then there was the singer . . . the guy wasn't trying to get your attention, he knew he had it, whether he did or not – whether you liked it or not. There was no way you would have been able to convince these guys that they weren't in total command. They got a mixed reaction between songs. The people who weren't going apeshit in their favor were doing so in the opposite direction. The point is, EVERYONE was going apeshit. By the end of the set, most of us in the crowd were soundly and sonically in favor of this young Southern Californian band with their first album out, still warm from the pressing plant.

Soon after their set was finished, The Motor City Madman took the stage. Something wasn't right. It was as if someone had come into his house and re-arranged all the furniture. Between songs the crowd started to chant the name of the opening band. At first The Nuge didn't seem to care. After a few more songs, the crowd was really going for it. Ted got pissed off, went up to the mic and screamed, 'FUCK VAN HALEN!!!' The rest of the gig was bullshit. Ted had kicked his own ass and he knew it. Van Halen had blown him off his own stage and they had so much fun doing it. You knew you had to go get that record so you could relive it in your room.

After that night, I became a big fan of the band and especially their singer, David Lee Roth. I read every interview I could find. The man never stopped smiling and never shut his mouth. He was always enjoying himself, or so it seemed. People I knew who didn't usually voice their opinions, always had an opinion about that guy. Either they were into Dave or they wanted to punch that grin right off his face. I could see why a lot of people hated his guts. His band kicked ass, he looked great, you knew that he was rich and getting down with beautiful women. He talked loud, he was funny and very smart. He knew that he was the ringmaster in the greatest show on earth. One thing that I knew infuriated people was that he was in such good physical shape but would never talk about the long hours of training it takes to build and maintain a body like that.

'I used to run but the ice kept falling out of my glass.' – This is basically saying that looking this great and kicking this much ass is no problem.

'What's the matter, aren't you having this much god-damn fun all the time? Cheer up!' This kind of thing can really piss some people off. 'Don't give me shit pal . . . I'll fuck your girlfriend!' The man is one of my heroes.

A few years after my introduction to Van and the Man, I was singing in a band myself. Dave became a different kind of inspiration because now it was I who got to go out and unleash the beast every night. I now understood where that big shit eating grin came from. It came from totally blowing all opening bands and audiences away. The hairier it gets, the wider you grin. Fuck 'em.

I used to get so much shit from people for being into the guy. People telling me that he was a clown, or that he was sexist. I always countered with my opinion that he was into being a showman and if he was down with the ladies, more power to him. Hell, I wish it was me. Sexist? Give me a break with that bullshit. People would ask me how I could identify with this guy. I told them that I identified with the rage in the music and the delivery. Looking around at what was happening then, you want to talk about rage and power, pure fury, the first Van Halen album makes Johnny Rotten out to be what he really was and still is, a hairdresser. While writing this article, the first VH CD is in its third play. That record is, I don't know how many years old, and it wipes the floor with most records coming out these days.

For several years, world tours and six awesome albums, Van Halen destroyed earth and everybody who went to the show had a damn good time. I know I did. Dave dressed the sets and choreographed all the moves. 'If all the world's a stage, then I want better lighting.' Their sixth record *1984* was their best seller. I played that one at hard volume this morning and yes, it makes ALL of these MTV dudes pale. Poison? I'm supposed to be into that? Get the fuck out of here.

Speaking of getting the fuck out, Roth quit Van Halen and from the interviews, it wasn't a very clean split. To say that there were some hard feelings would be approaching it. In the meantime, the band hired on a new singer, Sammy Hagar, one of the most incredible turn-offs known to mankind – diabolical.

Around the same time Dave split from the band, the band I was in broke up. I was either going to destroy or sink. Right on time, Dave's first solo album *Eat'em and Smile* hit the racks. It was a good shot in the arm. Soon I was in the studio doing my first solo record. I played Dave's record all the time. The first song on it is so great. 'Yankee Rose' – so crass and thunderous. '. . . *Guess who's back in circulation, now I don't know what you may have heard, but what I need right now is the original good time girl . . .*'

Dave was now the underdog, out on his own. The LP and Dave garnered all kinds of awards in Rolling Stone: Worst LP, Cover, Dressed and Male Vocalist. Awesome. Everybody had an opinion. It made me pull for him even more. I saw the tour, the second of two nights at the Inglewood Forum. It was so cool. He came out and introduced himself, 'LADIES AND GENTLEMEN, DAVID LEE ROTH!!!' and then fire, lights, explosions and the set started. What a crass motherfucker. What if you could do that kind of thing when you went into restaurants and funerals. Make no mistake, he and the band kicked ass that night.

Dave is part huckster, part Al Jolson. A song and dance man. He might not be on the cover of every rock magazine like he used to be, but no one lasts in that arena forever. He lasted longer and better than a lot of them. I am not going to name names, but looking at the trades and listening to what's out there, I think it best to leave the mag covers to these new guys who grew up listening to him. What the hell.

When I caught up with Dave, he was on a break from shooting film for his next video. Dave is high – high energy, high impact. He takes his fun seriously. 'Yes, I take what I do very seriously . . . it's what everybody thinks about what I'm doing that I don't take seriously.' At first, I was nervous about talking with him. That didn't last long though, he had me laughing too fast.

When not onstage or in the studio, Dave has been known to punctuate his life with voyages to distant locales to deal up close and personal with the terrain and its inhabitants. Such journeys include trips to New Guinea, the Amazon River and most recently, a trek through the Himalayas as well as a kayak mission in the South Pacific. These experiences give him a perspective that you might not get here in town. Take it Dave:

'Here in the city, not getting eaten by something is down around number twenty-eight on your priority list . . . when you're deep water kayaking in the South Pacific, not getting eaten is suddenly up around two or three . . . This is healthy.'

I ask Dave about the steaming jungles of New Guinea, where the paper on your passport rots right there in your hand. He told me about seeing a three day dance ceremony called a 'Sing-Sing', where tribes from all over come and try to outdance each other. It's a big throw-down, a party out in the jungle to see who has the scariest looking crew. Dave described it as 'Christmas and the Tet Offensive rolled into one'. After dealing with that for a few days where 'the breakfast of champions isn't cereal, it's the opposition', a stadium show in front of fifty thousand people is not really anything to get nervous about. *This* is perspective.

I hit Dave with a quote of his, a thing that I had been doing all night (I am a well-versed Rothologist).

'Dave, I read in an interview that you said your main motivation for performing was "Fear and revenge". That was a while ago, how about these days?'

'I was very competitive then, with the powers that be. I still make the joke which I got from John Wayne in *The Alamo*. "There's a lot of pretenders to the throne here, we can't stop them from coming on, but we can arrange for them to limp home." I always took that to heart. I had something to prove. There was a lot of rage there, a lot of fury, and a lot of fun and celebrations along the way. After a while I realized that I would never be happy unless I was doing it for myself and not doing things to compete, not even concerning myself with it because I don't consider myself a part of any specific musical group. It's not heavy metal, it's not pop, although there's elements of both. It's not purely vaudeville or big band yet those elements are intact. I used to be worried about what it is. Now I don't care, I guess it's the difference between the way Tom Selleck and Marlon Brando act. One is a result-oriented performance and the other is just being it.

'We take the Honda principle which is, "If two is good then five is better," and we go with the Cecil B. DeMille kind of vision, with a cast of thousands or as many as we can afford. Most of the characters in my films are passive, so you really are drawn into the scene. There are layers to it so you can watch these videos fifty times and find things in the background. It takes us a long time to put one of these together – roughly about a month and a half. You have one inspiration at 5:30 in the morning in some after-hours dive on the East Coast and you spend the next four and a half weeks getting up at 5:30 in the morning trying to make it transpire onto the screen just like you dreamt it between your ears or in your pants as the case may be – the visceral stuff's even harder to get up there.'

Dave and the band have been hitting the bricks almost every night, practicing over and over the songs that they will take on tour. 'It's a labor of love. If you're in this for things other than the music – and we're all in this for things other than the music . . . The guy who said that money can't buy happiness didn't know where to go shopping. I'm not ruling out greed and avarice at all. But if those things are higher up on the list for you than the music, the whole parade will pale for you in the hundredth hour of vocal practice.'

So where does this guy get off? Probably more often than most.

'My whole thing is based on – and this is for me, mind you – that you have to discipline yourself, and through this discipline will come some level of achievement, and from this achievement will come your pride. There's nothing else but pride in all of this. The money comes and goes, the women come and go – but your pride can remain. It's pride that gets John Lee Hooker up the hill. It's pride brought Muhammad Ali back. It got Quayle elected to Vice President. Absolutely I'm not a supporter there, but I can salute the pride.'

When the David Lee Roth band hit the road, they bring the gear: bicycles, cross-country skis, mountain climbing equipment.

'What we call it in the basement, in slang, is "expert sportsman, world class mountaineering athletic type", the medical term in Latin is "Fun-Hog". I'm not good at any of it, but hey, we do dozens of things. To me, music always has to look like it sounds. Whatever that means to you, it should transpire. I like to use a lot of knees and elbows.'

Dave relates how he and some of the crew go for long bike rides in cities on tour. They don't worry about remembering which way they went, they just go and when they are ready to quit, they call the hotel and get the courtesy van to bring them in. Sometimes Dave and Company have ended up in some 'hoods that made the hotels downright nervous. Many nights on the tour, Dave and a handful of fellow Fun-Hogs will get in his bus and drive overnight to the next town where they will hook up with local climbers and spend the time before soundcheck repelling off the local range. Sometimes they hit it five days straight. 'You're dropping dead, but hey, you did it.'

Our talk went from New Guinea to Erie, Pennsylvania, from mountain climbing to meeting James Brown, videos, all kinds of stuff. It was great. I left feeling good. I told the cab driver that I had just spent the evening hanging with Diamond Dave. The guy lit up, looked into the rearview and said, 'Day-veed Lee Roth! Cally-for-nee-ya gurr-ells!'

Originally appeared in DETAILS

FIRING INTO A CROWDED SHOPPING MALL

May 12, 1992/Madrid, Spain I was standing on the corner watching a store burn. The sun was setting and I could see the helicopters flying low overhead. People were running down the street with their arms full of looted goods. A rent-a-pig walked over from the record store he was guarding across the street to where myself and the other spectators were standing. He pointed across the street to where a few men were standing, holding rocks. He told us that these men were going to loot the record store. He then proceeded to try to convince us to line up in front of the record store window to make the looters back down. I considered the idea of taking a rock in the head for U2, getting my cranium crushed for Warrant. I decided it was a bad and worthless idea.

At that moment, I saw a young man put a trash can through the window of a liquor store. A few men behind me, armed with sticks ran after him. People behind me cheered and screamed.

'Get him, he's getting away!'

In my mind, they were all assholes. I went back inside my apartment so I wouldn't get killed or something.

A couple of days later I went to the airport via La Cienega Blvd. Stores burnt, cars burnt. Store windows with pictures of Martin Luther King pasted up as some kind of safeguard – as if it would make a difference. Destruction for miles and miles. I only saw one street. Los

Angeles has a lot of streets. I tried to calculate the total damage in my head – forget it.

I saw it – you saw it. The whole world saw Rodney King get the daylights beaten out of him. When the pigs went free, I thought to myself:

What do they need? A three camera shoot directed by De Palma? How much more graphic can you get?

Even this now famous video couldn't stop the LAPD.

The statement was made: the pigs answer to no one. They can do whatever they want. The United States is a white-run police state. If you don't like it, then change the channel.

The ghetto residents did exactly what they had been trained to do all their lives – destroy their own environment and each other, fall deeper into helpless rage, hatred and despair. The pigs had won again. Now all the powers that be can point and say, 'See, they're animals. They get what they deserve.' The drag is that a lot of people will believe this.

In no way am I saying that I think it's ok to wreck other people's property. But, if you show millions of people that you don't care about their lives and treat them like subhumans, a small portion of them will show you a thing or two as well.

America is a hard country to live in. The place breaks my heart. Hendrix, Miles, James Brown, Iggy, Coltrane – they all came from here. Hubert Selby, Fugazi, Chuck D. – you know what I mean. But at the same time, it murdered my best friend. I have bars on my windows. I walk the streets looking over my shoulder – like prison.

ISAAC HAYES

Isaac Hayes has been a major figure in music since he walked through the doors of Memphis, Tennessee based Stax Records in 1964 He started as a sideman on Otis Redding and Booker T. sessions. Soon after, he hooked up with David Porter and the two became one of the most noteworthy songwriting teams of their time. The two of them worked nonstop, cranking out music for Stax artists. Perhaps the team's most well-known efforts were 'Soul Man' and 'Hold On, I'm Coming', the latter being one of the first number one hits for Stax.

Ike went solo in 1969 with his first album *Presenting Isaac Hayes*, which didn't do all that well. 1971 saw the release of his second album, *Hot Buttered Soul* which sold over a million copies. Soon after followed *The Movement*, *To Be Continued*, *Shaft* and *Black Moses*. All of these titles sold well over a million each. *Shaft* got him an Oscar.

I was introduced to Ike's music when I was in the fifth grade. My mother had some of his records. I used to listen to *Shaft* and *Hot Buttered Soul*. I don't know why, but at an early age I connected with these records. I dragged them to my room and they never left. I eventually took her other Ike records and wore them out. When I was older, I bought them again. To this day, I still play them.

Rappers have been making records out of his records for years. Check out Public Enemy's use of 'Hyperbolicsyllabicsesquedalymistic' on 'Black Steel in the Hour of Chaos'.

Ike has just made his best record in years. It's called *Branded*. For these sessions he went back down to Memphis, brought in members of the Bar-Kays and the Memphis Horns and did the whole thing the old way. The record has some of the most honest sounds and confident playing I have heard in a while. He re-did two of his older songs. 'Hyperbolic' gets another run-through with the addition of some vocals by Chuck D., as well as a song that should have been a classic the first time around, 'Soul-sville', from the *Shaft* album. He got together with David Porter for the first time in about twenty years and they wrote a song for the record called 'Thanks to the Fool'. There is an instrumental album to follow called *Raw and Refined*.

I interviewed the man briefly in Los Angeles in February 1995. It was great to hang out with someone I have been a fan of for so many years. He was a friendly and articulate man. I had a cool time. I'll get out of the way and let Ike rap.

About the rap on 'By the Time I Get to Phoenix' . . .
Well, it was out of the necessity to communicate. I'll give you the story. When I first heard the tune by Glen Campbell, I was knocked out. And the guy that wrote it, I thought, that guy really must have loved this woman. So, I wanted to do the song. Nobody had my enthusiasm. There was a nightclub in Memphis called The Tiki Club and we all hung out there in different groups. The Bar-Kays were playing. So I said, 'Hey man, I'm coming down tonight to sit in with you guys,' and I said, 'Learn "Phoenix".' So they learned the song and when I got up on the stage, everybody was talking. I thought, 'Damn, I gotta

get their attention!' And the first chord, I do believe that first chord was b flat eleven. I said, 'Hang up on that chord, man. Just keep cycling it.' And I started talking. I had to do something to get their attention so I started telling a story of what would have preceded him saying, 'By the time I get to Phoenix.' And halfway through my talking, the conversation subsided. People were listening. I thought, 'Damn! I got 'em!' And I went on telling my story. When got to the opening line, 'By the time . . .', the response was like, wow! And before the end of the song, people were crying and woeing and involved in it. I did the same thing at a predominately white club, same response. A DJ named Scott Shannon, who is now in NYC said, 'Isaac, man, you need to record that song!' So when I had the opportunity, I did.

Is the version on the record live?
Yeah. I was sitting at the organ and you can tell because in the end of the song in the back we were just jamming out. I was raking my hands on the keys and you can hear my fingernails hitting the keys, coming through my vocal mic. So, yeah – we did it live one time through.

There's been a lot of Ike samples out there in the rap world . . .
Well, a lot of my stuff has been sampled by so many rappers. I mean, I was with Scarface the other day, and he's in a lot of stuff with the Ghetto Boys and his solo act. Ice-T, Kool Moe Dee, Daddy Kane, L.L. Cool J, Eazy E . . . You just name 'em and they did my stuff. I went to the place that administers the publishing. Man, they showed me the printouts . . .

Are you getting publishing credits on this? I know some guys pay and some guys don't.
Yeah, but the guys that don't, they pay (laughs). They're penalized if they don't.

Yeah, they oughta!
The publishing administrator can demand all if they want to.

When I was growing up, you and Muhammad Ali were two of the most prominent black men in the media. With all the power that you had in the music industry and the black community, do you think you ever imposed a threat to the status quo or power structure?
I was held back – especially in the business. A lot on TV because I looked militant. And they equated me with black militants at the time because of the look. I was very, very militant because having brought up myself under those conditions and speaking out when I felt like injustice was done. I fought for a lot of causes – equal opportunity, equal housing, equal employment. I was always outspoken in the trenches. I was a lifetime member of the NAACP. I was, still am. I used to do gigs on college campuses with the black students union. Did a lot for the United Negro College Fund and all these things. But it was in the struggle and during the sixties and seventies, you know, black consciousness was up there as far as the struggle, and I was in that. So a lot of places I was not welcome. And there were threats quite a bit. But it didn't stop me because I was committed. But they didn't let me on TV a lot. Because my appearance changed with the bare chest and all that kind of stuff, they said, 'No, we can't do that.

It's too much.' So, I missed out on a lot of opportunities because of that. Because of the decision of the status quo. That, hey, this guy shouldn't be allowed to do this and do that because of my . . . and my political views as well. You know, I spoke out on a lot of things like that. I was instrumental in getting a few African-American people elected to run for office on a local, state and national level. And when I did that, it was considered an affront as far as the status quo was concerned. So yeah, I created some turbulence.

How Porter and Hayes wrote 'Hold On I'm Coming' . . .
You've probably heard this story. Starts in a big of room like a movie theater. It was divided into studio A and we hadn't even opened B yet. The toilet was up in the corner of the room. I'm sitting in the center of the room, up against the wall by the piano, playing. And Dave said, 'Man, I've got to go to the john.' He went to the restroom, and I struck a groove. And I said, 'Damn. I don't want to lose this thing . . . HEY MAN! C'MON, MAN!' And he said, 'HOLD ON, I'M COMING!' And he came out the john with his pants down saying, 'That's it! That's it! Man, I got the title! I got the title!' And hey, we sat down and wrote 'Hold On I'm Coming'. You know, it's a funny thing the way these tunes come about.

Where did you get the ideas for the incredible arrangements that you did?
What happened was – during my formative years, I always loved music. I grew up in a musical family. I loved all kinds of music – blues, jazz, country, gospel, pop. I used to love Nat Cole, Perry Como, Tony Bennett. I used to love

to listen to all those songs. I used to sing them in high school, when I was in elementary school. You sing in contests and stuff. Now I was absorbing all of these influences. When time came for me to do my creative thing the way I wanted to do it without someone telling me how I should do it, then I started to stretch. Jim Stewart – he always wanted simple changes. 1-3-5. That was it. Marvell Thomas, Rufus' son, Carla's brother. He and I would play the keyboard and we would sometimes add a major seven and he would say, 'I don't want that pretty stuff. GIMMIE SOME FUNK!' I felt very inhibited but, when it was time for me to do my thing, I then said, 'Ok. Now I can do what I wanna do!' And I started stretching out. But I maintained musical integrity as far as R&B was concerned, by keeping it funky and having a lot of rhythm and so forth. And you can see flavors of classical music because I used to love classical music. I took music in high school, and I took music appreciation about Beethoven, Debussy, Strauss and all of these people. And I loved it! I had no formal training to execute or play it or write it, but I loved it. So again, that was one of the ingredients that went into my music.

If you listened to the string arrangement on 'Walk On By' . . . I just had a chance to really stretch out because when I did *Hot Buttered Soul*, Al Bell told me that twenty-six LPs had to be completed for a sales meeting in spring. And he said, 'I want you to help me produce some of these,' and I said, 'Ok, and by the way, can I do mine too?' And he said yeah. Now this was after my initial album called *Presenting Isaac Hayes*. I said, 'Can I do it the way I want to?' He said, 'Yeah, you got carte blanche.' He untied my hands and I felt no pressure because if there's twenty-five or twenty-six other LPs, then hey, I can do what I want and I don't have to worry about carrying a load. That gave me a chance to stretch out with these arrangements and be artistically free. That's when I did the arrangement on 'Walk On By'. Something in me said, if you cover somebody's tune, if you do it verbatim, it will be boring. If the tune was already a hit, how are you going to have any success standing in the shadow of that? A hit song is a hit song – it will stand the test of time. So what I did was, I dissected it and put it back together the way I felt comfortable with. That's the way 'Walk On By' came out. I added these strings onto it and guitar underneath it. By my not having any formal training, I didn't have any of the restrictions and the dos and don'ts of music which leaves one to be innovative. There were no boundaries.

On *Black Moses* . . .
I started working on *Black Moses* before *Shaft* came out. Now if you notice the titles of the tunes . . . I was going through a marriage breakup. I was going through hell. Think about it: 'Never Gonna Say Goodbye', 'Never Going To Give You Up', 'Nothing Takes The Place Of You', 'I Need To Belong To Someone', 'I'll Never Fall In Love Again', 'Help Me Love', 'Gotta Find Me A Part Time Love'. All these tunes were depicting the hell I was living in at the time.

On drugs . . .
The whole thing is a condition created by a racist society. This is the by-product. It started years ago. It started when our forefathers came off the ships as captives. Give the situation that a black man was not allowed to be a man,

whenever he stood up and spoke for his family, the Klan would take him outside, beat him and lynch him. So he had to stop being a man for fear of his life or the welfare of his family. That put the black woman in the forefront. She was safe so she could be the mother of the whole house which degraded the father figure and the husband figure in the household. It became perpetual. Then when he didn't work because he was afraid to or didn't speak up, he was called lazy. Then growing up in a racist environment where you have Negro history once a year, one week – Negro History Week when I was a kid. You allow these kids only one week a year for them to learn about themselves. That's not enough. If you've been beat over the head for years, being told that you are inferior, that you are nothing, that everything black is negative – Black Tuesday, black sheep, black lie – all these black connotations lead to negativity. Kids are going to start thinking that way. The heroes were all white. Cowboys were white, Santa Claus was white, Tarzan was white. Kids started saying, 'I don't want to be black.' When I was growing up and I was called black in the 'hood, those were fighting words. Then came the civil rights struggle, the sixties and the Vietnam war and the protests, and blacks were protesting for their equal rights. When the smoke cleared, desegregation started to happen. Some had jobs, some didn't. Then came the drugs in the neighborhood – heavily. The status quo said I don't give a damn about that, let them kill themselves. They couldn't get jobs. It was frustrating. A lot of guys went off to the service and risked their lives for their country and came back – no equal employment. So what do you do? You turn to drugs as an escape because you're in denial about that situation.

Entertainers who do drugs have a problem. They are not living up to their responsibilities. When you achieve notoriety, there's a responsibility that goes with it because you're bigger than life in the eyes of your fans. So what you do is legitimate. So if you do it, then they figure that it's alright for them to do it. The ones who do the drugs have to be more responsible because whatever you do, it's going to influence someone.

After a lot of drug programs were cut out by the government, by certain administrations, then these kids had no recreational things in the evening to keep them occupied. And as the saying goes, 'An idle mind is the devil's workshop.' When suppressed by a society, racist or otherwise, you tend to strike out at the ones who are closest to you. If you have a house and your family is a happy, loving family and you hit a financial crisis and there's not enough money around, tempers get short and you yell at the ones that you love and don't really mean it. In the black neighborhoods, when there's no way out, you start taking your frustrations, your misplaced hostilities, out on the person that's nearest you. And in order to survive, if they aren't going to give you any money, or a job, then you're going to get it the best way you can. You think you're surviving.

None of this became a crisis until it spilled out into other areas. When white kids started doing drugs, then there was a drug problem. Nancy Reagan started putting on all these campaigns fighting drugs. Somebody makes money from drugs. The kids don't manufacture them – it has to come in from somewhere. The real guys who need to be in jail are the ones in the suits who deal this stuff from high office buildings. The effect is in the 'hood. And with lack of education, that's the only way they know how to survive. Some kids have already accepted the fact that they have a life expectancy of no more than twenty-two or twenty-five years so they figure that's it. That's the condition that they're living in. And that is why we who are of note should try to do something to turn this around.

If the status quo had allowed African studies into the curriculum, if it was compulsory learning, we would have a different opinion about ourselves – a sense of history, a sense of belonging – and the kids of other racial ethnicities would have known about us. There would not have been the ignorance which breeds fear which breeds hatred. It would have been wiped out a long time ago.

When you try to do some good in an area, there are some people who consider that a threat to their well-being and they will do all they can to stop it. That's what we're dealing with. I am dedicated to making a change for the better. We're all on this planet and we have to live together. If we are to go into the next millennium, we have to get it together or there will be nothing left for the kids. That is my goal. And to do it through music and communication and the arts, I will do what I can to make a difference for the better on this planet. Hats off to people like to Chuck D. for doing what he does. Through the arts, we can be very effective. The arts cross through all barriers, lines and languages. Music is more important than just for pleasure. You can communicate. That's why so much responsibility goes along with the notoriety that people in the arts and athletes have.

Originally appeared in RAYGUN

JOHN LEE HOOKER

In interviews, John Lee Hooker is a man of few words
He answers politely and succinctly, which leads the
interviewer (this time me) tempted to smile, nod encourag-
ingly and say, 'Yes, and . . .' He's one of those guys who
doesn't have to say anything. His music speaks volumes.
He's a blues man. If you have to ask, then you're never
going to know, as they say. Knowing this, I prepared my
questions carefully, wanting to stay ten miles away from
anything that remotely resembled 'Johnny, what's the
blues?' I've seen him asked that question before and I have
seen him really try to explain what cannot be explained. It
must be a drag to be tossed that one a few times a week
for a few decades. I saw a short film on Lightnin' Hopkins
years ago where the interviewer asked him what the blues
were and Lightnin', by way of reply, started doing these
amazing runs on the guitar that was sitting on his lap.
Worked for me.

For the millionth time, John Lee Hooker was born in
Mississippi, August 22, 1920 says the Virgin press release.
1917 says the great music writer Robert Palmer in his book
Deep Blues. 'Somebody knows,' says Hooker. He ended up
in Detroit by the early forties and it was there that he made
his first recordings. In 1948, he recorded some songs as a
demo for Bernie Bessman and the west coast label, Modern
picked 'Boogie Chillun' as a single. It sold over a million
copies. John quit his factory job and took the music angle
a bit more seriously. A single that followed, 'I'm in the
Mood' was an even bigger hit. Several hits came after that

– 'Crawling Kingsnake', 'One Bourbon, One Scotch, One Beer' – the list goes on.

His multi-decade career has seen many ups and downs, mostly with the tides and trends of popular music. He has maintained a great and long friendship with Van Morrison whom he has toured and recorded with on several occasions. He did a lot of work with Canned Heat, who owe a lot to Hooker's sound for their better recordings. In fact, the Canned Heat boys probably owe a lot of people. They had a big hit many years ago, 'Goin' Up the Country', a great melody line, very memorable. Really memorable when I heard Worried Henry Thomas' 'Bulldoze Blues' recorded years before the Heat boys were even born. They ripped the song off note for note and slightly changed a few lyrics and lived high on the hog off the proceeds. So, to hell with those guys.

If you've never heard Hooker play, you might have missed your chance in the live capacity as he has gone into semi-retirement, but his better records hold up brilliantly. There's nothing like the John Lee Hooker sound. I remember the first time I heard his album *That's Where It's At!* The haunting, droning hollow body guitar, the sound of his heel tapping on a pinewood plank and the depth of his voice made me think he came from another planet. He sang about floods, funerals, women leaving, waiting for them to come back. I would get caught up in the sadness and then on the next track, he would turn the mood around and let the boogie rip with some smokin' uptempo stomp. All done with a unique sound from another eon. His music had absolutely nothing to spare. Everything that he played and sang was essential. I was a fan immediately.

Chill Out (Pointblank/Virgin) is the title of his new record and it is a great one. Who knows how many records he has done at this point. One might be hesitant to check out a contemporary recording of a man who goes back so far and you would do yourself a favor to check out his Vee Jay, United Artists and other early recordings. BUT, *Chill Out* burns. Producer Roy Rogers retains what is great about the Hooker sound and the musicians that he brings to the session lets you know that he knows what serious music is all about, and they give it up big time. Hanging out with Hooker on the new album are such greats as Carlos Santana, Van Morrison, Charles Brown, Danny Caron and Staxman Booker T. Jones.

So I get a call asking if I want to interview John Lee Hooker for *Huh?* magazine. About fifty of his records sit against one wall, live tapes I got through trades and one I made myself from one of the three times I've seen him play sit on a shelf across the room. I stopped writing for *Spin* magazine several years ago after reading an article about him that was so wrong-headed that even Hooker wrote in about it. It seemed like a good opportunity to turn it around. Off to one of his pieces of property, a nice spread in Long Beach, I went.

I was told that his place would be hot by one of the Point Blank people on the way there. We walked into his place and it was hot as a furnace. John was sitting on the couch, in a suit, watching the OJ trial. He was wearing those funky star-spangled socks that I have seen him wear in so many pictures of him.

One of my favorite recordings that you've done was the collaboration with Earl Palmer, Taj Mahal and Miles

Davis for *The Hot Spot* soundtrack. What was it like working with Miles?
He was great. He said, 'Johnny, this is so beautiful. You're the funkiest man alive.' And he gave me a big hug.

I saw you on video sitting next to Carlos Santana playing a version of 'Red House' recently. Did you ever meet Hendrix? Were you aware of his music?
Oh yes, I was very aware of his music. People told me he wanted to meet with me but we never got the chance.

One of my favorite songs I've seen you play is 'I Cover the Waterfront'. When did you start playing that, a long time ago?
Yeah.

The first time I saw you play it was in 1985 at McCabe's.
Oh yeah, McCabe's. That place is still goin'. Old guitar shop.

Which do you prefer, playing with the band or by yourself?
I like both really. But I can get a lot deeper playing by myself. I don't have to think about being too loud or to do this or do that. I've been thinking about doing a whole album on my own.

That's how you started out.
That's right, just by myself. I love that old stuff. It's the real McCoy.

How did you get that sound?
I got it from my stepfather. (*Will Moore, it is said, played with Charlie Patton.*)

What people were you going to see when you were coming up?
T-Bone Walker. He was my favorite on the electric guitar. He's one of the greatest musicians alive I think.

Has the meaning of music changed for you over the years?
I've seen it come and I've seen it go. Different styles. But I never changed. I wouldn't dare to try to tempt it. To change John Lee Hooker would lose the feeling. That wouldn't be me.

What kept you going back on stage for so many years?
Not the money. I love people and people love me, I know that. As long as people want to see me do my thing, I'll do it. I do a lot of benefits, get money to people.

When you went to England to play a long time ago, the Rolling Stones were your opening band.
Yeah, they were just kids.

You have made a lot of friends over the years. Who are some of the people who mean a lot to you?
Bonnie Raitt, Carlos Santana, Van Morrison.

When did you meet Van Morrison?
About twenty years ago. He came to one of my shows. He can sing the blues. He's the greatest in the world. He's hard to get to know.

Intense?
Very intense.

Have you been doing a lot of interviews since the new record is out?
Yes. A lot. Too many.
(*I see my interview opportunity starting to dwindle.*)

The blues is the deepest music there is. It's eternal. Being such a part of it, I think that you become eternal yourself. Like Coltrane.
Yes. He's gone but he's still here. Like me and the rest of them, we're still going to be here. It lives on. What's his name . . . at the crossroads?

Robert Johnson?
Yeah, he's still here. I never did meet him neither.

A lot of people have been influenced by your style – ZZ Top, for instance.
Yeah, he really cleaned up. I don't care though.

George Thorogood.
Yeah, he started out by playing John Lee Hooker music. He told me, 'You made me who I am.' I said, 'Yeah I know.' I love George.

How do you see yourself in the big picture of music?
I see myself as a loving human being. I got a lot to offer people. I have given so much to people and have gotten so much back and I'm proud.

What is it like to have played so long and be so old and have everybody think you're cool? Because they do, you know that.

I love people. I meet as many of them as I can. I can't meet them all, but I meet them all in spirit. They are the ones who made me.

Your music never sounds dated. It sounds like it has always been here and will always be here. I guess you don't think about time. You just get to the music and play it.

No, I don't think about time. You're here when you're here. I think about today, stay in tune.

We talk about musicians who follow trends and get lost in the shuffle.

I write songs that have meaning to them. Mostly about women.

Don't we all.

(He breaks out laughing.) You can't leave them out!

Sometimes you wish you could, though!

Yeah! You can for a few hours and then they come right back. Boom!

Originally appeared in HUH?

LOLLAPALOOZA TOUR JOURNAL

7.17.91 2:04 p.m. En route to Phoenix AZ The last few days were loaded to say the least. Sunday, we played outside in Princeton with Ween. It was a free show. Good to get in a show before we do the tour. Would have been even better to have been able to have played a week of shows. After the show, we found out that while we were playing, someone had opened the hood of the van and ripped out all the wires around the engine. We did get it back together again thanks to Mickey Ween. After that, Haskett and I had to take the gear to the freighting place in NYC. Didn't get home until late.

Met with Alan Vega the other day at his place in NYC. It was great. He's such a cool guy. We talked for a few hours in his living room. He gave me a copy of his new CD. Of course, he can't get a deal in this country. How typical. He had some great stories. He said that seeing the Stooges play was the greatest musical statement he ever saw. He gave me a book of pictures and writing that came out in Japan. It's awesome, really great. He told me about doing the second Suicide album down the hall from Bruce Springsteen and how he is a big fan of the band. Alan has had a hard time with the record business over the last few years. All of the masters for his solo albums were sitting in a pile in his living room near his stereo. What a trip.

11:16 p.m.: At the hotel in Phoenix. Worked out in the gym here. It's supposed to be 106 degrees onstage tomorrow. I can't wait to hit it. I've been waiting for this for some time now.

7.18.91 3:00 p.m. Phoenix AZ We got onstage for soundcheck at ten in the morning and it was already in the nineties. The show went ok. Hot as hell onstage by the time we finally got on there. The mic wasn't on for the first part of the first song but it still rocked. I must have looked funny, singing, looking all into it, and no sound coming out. A great way to start out the entire tour. I did an interview with the guy from MTV. That was a great old time. I was just giving him all this shit I could come up with and he didn't get it. Joe videotaped the whole thing.

When Nine Inch Nails were onstage, something went wrong with their equipment and the band broke some of their stuff and stormed off. We were in our dressing room with some of the Jane's guys, just laughing at their attitude. I met Ice-T and Vernon Reid, they were cool. This should be a good trip.

I'm flying back to LA tonight as I have a day off tomorrow.

7.21.91 12:10 a.m. LA CA Did the show in San Diego today. Same place I saw the Dead in '85. Today was rockin'. The air was cool and it was general seating so everybody was up front. Ice-T watched the whole set. He and the rest of the Syndicate guys are cool. Had to do a few interviews and meet the faceless radio people who tell you that they have met you three times before and you can never remember. Talked with Gibby and King from the Butthole Surfers. They were telling me about hanging out with Roky Erickson in Austin where they all live and had some interesting stories about him. Roky Erickson is amazing. I never met anyone who actually met him.

Got back here a few hours ago. Have to get up in the morning and go to Irvine for the first of three shows there.

Ice-T was kicking today. It's good that we go on before them, I get to see them play and not have to think about going on. I'm tired from the workout that I did and the show and the whole day.

7.21.91 9:14 p.m. LA CA Just got back from the first of the three Irvine shows. When we went on at two p.m., there was hardly anyone there. Most of the audience were about fifty yards away in the field at the top of the hill. It was like playing alone in the middle of a parking lot, but it was cool anyway. It's frustrating when a ton of people show up thirty minutes after we play though. When Ice goes on, there's a load of people. He and his guys were great today, the best they've been yet. Ice-T said some funny shit out there today.

'Henry Rollins, the baddest motherfucker in the world was out here playing and you all watched him like he was Bob Hope!'

Tomorrow is a day off. In the evening, Hubert Selby and Don Bajema are coming over and we're going to tape a few hours of spoken word onto a DAT player I got. It's this 'Three Men In A Room' idea that I had a few weeks ago. The three of us sitting in a room, each taking turns reading stuff or talking or whatever. It sounds like a good idea but we'll see how it goes.

I'm tired and trying to get all the shit together so I can get out of here and not have it all fuck up on me. It's good to be in my room. Strange to come here after a band show. I got up early this morning and worked out. I'm pretty beat.

7.23.91 1:24 a.m. LA CA Tonight we did the recording. Selby came over and Don flew down from SF. The taping went pretty well I think. All three of us sat in front of the mic and kicked it for ninety-five minutes or so. I played some of it back and it's good. Have to get up early and get in a workout before we go out to Irvine. No real sleep until the day off in San Francisco.

I must keep up the work. I am getting close to finishing a lot of the things that I started a few years ago. For the rest of the tour I must be steady and resourceful. I must not neglect writing. I must take advantage of every moment to work.

7.23.91 11:14 p.m. LA CA The second Irvine show is finished, better than yesterday's. We played a different set as well. Still, there was the drag of playing to no one but that's the way it is being the opening band. *We are the band that plays as the audience is in traffic or puking on their shoes in the parking lot.* Ice-T seemed like he was in a bad mood today when he got to the stage. Don't know, maybe he was just being quiet. We did a photo shoot for *Rolling Stone.* The guy was finished with us in two minutes. Talked to Alex Winter who did that *Bill and Ted's Excellent Adventure* film. He says the sequel is doing ok. Did an interview with *Spin,* that was all of five minutes. I don't think they wanted to talk to me. Worked out this morning. Will do the same tomorrow morning. Tonight will be last night I spend in my own bed for a long time. I am making as many tapes as I can, have been for the last few days. I'm looking forward to getting out of here. How many times have I said that? I know that the playing will get better when I'm away from home. I don't play well unless I am well away from where I live.

It will be interesting to see how all the bands play three weeks from now. We'll see if anyone burns out. Somehow

LOLLAPALOOZA TOUR JOURNAL

I don't see the Nine Inch Nails guys sticking for the whole thing. I don't know why I get that feeling. Looking forward to playing tomorrow.

7.25.91 1:04 a.m. En route to Mountain View CA Played well today. I had a good time. No one was there for our set. Ice-T introduced me to the Boo Ya Tribe guys this evening. Those are some big guys, really cool though. They look like they could benchpress cars. I talked to Flea while we watched Living Colour. He told me about going to Costa Rica. It's funny how the crowd responds to LC. They don't seem to know what to do with them. The band will be playing full-on and the crowd just stands there.

I got in a good workout while we waited to get out. It's great to hit the weights while Siouxsie plays. They make me want to kill, so it goes great. It's hard to be backstage when all the other bands are playing. I see them and it makes me want to go out and blow them off the stage and show them what the deal is. Later on in the day when the big bands are playing, the backstage is crawling with hot looking women who look at me with amusement. It's no big deal. To me, they're not real anyway. None of these people have anything to do with me or my world.

7.25.91 7:15 p.m. Mountain View CA Day off today. We drove in the bus after the show and got here early in the morning. I slept for a while and didn't remember where I was. Spent today typing and listening to music.

I talked to our manager Gail briefly. She will be coming up to the show tomorrow. She says that the guys in the band have money gripes and problems with Andy Wallace producing the next recording. The bass player has a lot of ideas as to how it all should be done. He always has a lot of ideas as to how things should be done. I have seen him in action. He produces by taking all his hilarious insecurities into the studio with him. I don't want another record that sounds like *Hard Volume*. It's a good record, but I want something different. That's why the outside producer.

Sometimes the attitudes of the band members make me mad. It takes me a few days and then I get over it, but sometimes I just feel like treating them like employees. I get resentful and I don't want to be emotionally involved with their lives. It takes too much time and it's not always worth it. I feel that they think I'm up to something or trying to rip them off. They want more money? Fine. I'll see what I can do. They want things more business like? That's fine by me. Let's see if they can hack it. When the next record comes out and we are playing every night, I don't want to hear one fucking peep out of them that they're tired or whatever. I don't give a fuck. One of the things that causes friction is that I'm not a musician and I do my best to keep that in mind. I guess I wish that sometimes they were a little tougher. Some of the things that come out of their mouths make me laugh. I don't think they could have hacked it in the Flag. Whatever. It really doesn't matter does it?

So now it's evening. Einsturzende Neubauten is playing in town tonight. The others are going. I am not. There might be some people at the show that I shouldn't see. Also, I have to work out tonight. It's not good to be near people when I should be working. A lot of the guys in the bands are soft. They're scammers – looking good for the camera and getting their little stage act together. It's so weak. None of them play with the taste of blood in their mouths. I feel nothing in common with hardly anyone in the bands on this bill. It's show biz for them. It never gets real.

7.27.91 12:29 a.m. Mountain View CA Had a good time playing today. The place is great. The Shoreline Amphitheater is owned by Bill Graham. He ran around all day making sure that all was going ok. The food was great. Again, no one was there to see us but we're used to that by now.

Tom Waits was in Jane's Addiction's dressing room tonight. I talked to him for a while. What a cool guy. He was talking about how people are 'bone machines'. I'm tired from the playing and the length of time outside. I'll write more when I get the chance.

7.28.91 11:07 a.m. Somewhere in Nevada We drove after the show. Good to be out of California. No shows for a couple of days as we will be driving to Kansas. This will be good. Hopefully now the tour will get real. No pretty girls backstage. The bands won't have their friends around to kiss their ass and they'll have to let the music do the talking. We'll see who sticks to the wall and who falls off.

I got into this thing with this girl backstage in San Francisco. She came up and started talking a line of bullshit to me, feeling me up and asking me where I was going after the show. I told her I wanted to cut her head off and do art with her blood. We went to check out the Banshees set and she tried to get me to go into a women's room stall with her. I couldn't see myself trying to fuck some girl in a room full of girls pissing. She gave me her number and told me to come check her out whenever I was in her neck of the woods. I threw the number out. I liked the idea of her going to the trouble of writing it out when I knew all the while I was going to toss it.

11:43 p.m.: Still driving, don't know where we are. The front of the bus is alright – nice chairs, good lighting. We got some Elmore James on the stereo. This isn't bad.

It's good to get out of LA. Good to be away from the girl that I have been seeing lately. I have no problems with her. It's just that I know I'm better off on my own when I don't have to consider anyone else outside of a professional capacity. Affection has no place when I am on tour. It's best when I don't have to be a human being. I am finding it harder and harder to deal with people. They piss me off a lot of times. I don't think I am cut out for a close relationship with a woman. It gets to a certain point then I just switch off. I don't know why yet.

7.29.91 11:02 p.m. Kansas City KS I woke up this morning at about five with the smell of sulfur in my lungs. My head was pounding and my ears were ringing. The whole bus stank of it. As it happens, the batteries had dried up and the gas was coming into the bus through the air vents. We pulled over to the side of the road. We put a few gallons of water into the batteries. I did my best not to puke from the headache. No one else even woke up. We got here in the early afternoon. Dave, the driver, did the whole thing without sleeping, about forty hours straight.

Did four interviews on the phone thirty minutes after we got into the rooms. One of the guys tried to fuck with me but I got him good. He said that by answering the questions with few words I was being evasive. I told him that I could fill him up with bullshit and say things that would make him feel good about himself or things that would make him blow his fucking brains out, but instead of that bullshit, I was giving him the straight answers. Fuck these people.

After that, I went to this radio station and talked to these two guys on the air for a while. They were cool, funny as shit and they let me do what I wanted.

Now back at the hotel. A few kids were in the lobby. Apparently, the hotel has sold out all the rooms. Most of them went to kids that have traveled many miles to see the show tomorrow.

Chris is gone somewhere and I'm alone in the room. It's good. I have been thinking about the writing that I want to start doing. I have cut away all the fat tissue, now it's time to get to the bone and start hacking. The rest of the things that I have to say will be fucked. It's all down to rage and bitterness. The truth as I see it. Pure death all the way. I want to be straight up. I'll probably be hated for it but I don't care. Good thing we're playing tomorrow. I don't think I could take another day on that bus.

7.30.91 6:22 p.m. Kansas City KS I'm in the dressing room putting up with Nine Inch Nails. These guys are so weak it's not funny. Ice-T was so great today. We don't leave for hours yet. Our set was ok. I felt the days off. Workout was hard today as well. I'm going to hit it some more later. Did a few interviews. Pretty lame people they put in front of me – so weak. Other than that, there's nothing here. The drag is that after we're finished playing it only feels like soundcheck. When Ice-T is on, I want to play. This will be a frustrating tour in that way. Tonight, we drive to St. Paul, MN. Tomorrow is a day off. I will try to get in a run while marooned there. Pretty boring day today, didn't get much out of the set. It was so hot onstage with the sun on top of us that I couldn't concentrate. I just tried not to puke. People seemed to have a good time.

7.31.91 12:15 p.m. St. Paul MN Left the show last night right after Jane's Addiction finished playing.

A fucked up thing happened yesterday. I was standing by myself and this girl came up to me and asked me what I do. Wanting to avoid what I thought was coming, I told her that I was a lighting technician. I was hoping that she would find me uninteresting and leave me alone. It didn't work. She hit on me anyway. I steered her off this conversation, sat her down and talked to her. I told her that she didn't have to have sex with guys all the time just to have them as friends. I told her that she should stop hurting herself like this. She seemed to agree with me.

She seemed like a cool girl, kind of plain but very nice. Later on, she was in a trailer having sex with people from some of the bands. I watched people go in and out. After a while, all of them had gone and she came staggering out, wiping her mouth on her jacket. She saw me and looked down. She walked through the parking lot and disappeared.

Today is a day off in St. Paul. Don't know what I will do with myself outside of writing. The hotel is downtown, near the place we're playing tomorrow. I'm not tired. Maybe some coffee is in order.

1:42 a.m.: I talked briefly to one of Jane's Addiction's managers. Listening to him talk about how they go about things makes me see that I don't have any kind of real business sense at all. It's not like the guy is some kind of sleazy bastard, quite the opposite in fact. It's just that they have it all so together in ways that I never thought of. Thinking of how big that band is, I see now that it's a lot more than just the music that got them where they are. There's a lot of planning and wise moves made. Timing is a key element. I have no sense of that shit at all. I just assume you release everything you've ever done at once, play your guts out, give all, and you'll be alright. In a way, you will. You might not get rich, but that's ok. At least you will know that you gave it everything you had. There's no way that Jane's Addiction play every show like it was their last one. I have definitely seen them walk through one or two. Most bands do. It doesn't matter what they do. It only matters that I do my best out there every day, no matter what.

8.2.91 3:24 p.m. Got here several hours ago. We drove last night from St. Paul. I slept a little when I got in. Woke up to find that I had a nice long list of interviews to do and then I have less than an hour before I go into town and do a spoken show in Chicago. There's a day off on the tour and I'm working. Fine with me. What am I going to do with a night off?

I shouldn't have slept when I got here. It fucked me up. Two interviews down and I'm still spaced out. I am sinking into another depression. Sometimes I can't take it. All the thoughts I can muster to fight it off still can't stop it. Sometimes even the Part Animal, Part Machine mindset is of no help. I don't know what makes me get into this state. All I know is that I have to do a show tonight and all I want to do is shoot myself in the head.

1:01 a.m. at the hotel: Had a good time at the show. People were great as usual. I talked about John Macias. I told them about my pal Louie who overdosed and died recently. Talked about LA pigs. A lot of anti-drug stuff. A good time was had by all. I miss doing spoken shows. I will try to get more of them happening when I get the chance. With all the band stuff that's happening right now, I'm not getting to it like usual. Don't feel as depressed as I did before I left. Time to sleep. Another show lies ahead. All I want to do is hit it.

8.3.91 7:07 p.m. Chicago IL I was not pleased with the set today. It never really took off. Not that the guys were playing bad or anything, sometimes it just doesn't ignite. The crowd stood there and didn't move an inch. In fact, they looked bored. The best was the two guys with NIN shirts on laughing at me. I imagine I must look funny to their fans.

NIN have added another person to their tech crew, which means another person on the bus. He's alright, it's just that there wasn't a great deal of space in the first place and now we add another guy. Whatever.

Tomorrow is a show in Detroit. We did that city with JA before so it should be cool. Will be good to get on the road tonight and get out of here. Saw Al Jorgensen walking around the place today. I bet he's long gone. I would like to get him into a fight. It would keep me from getting bored, would make some people bum out, especially that scumbag.

Did too many interviews today. The first one started when I was in the shower at the hotel. I wasn't too good today. On the last one, all I talked about was Ted Bundy.

I asked the woman, who was getting on my nerves anyway, if she had any sisters and if I could hack their bodies into pieces. Oh well.

8.4.91 11:21 p.m., Detroit MI In the bus listening to Monk. We played good today. Just kicked the shit out of it. I went down in front and watched Ice-T and Body Count. They were great. Ice was funny as shit. He told this one girl to get up off her fat ass and the whole place laughed. At one point, Ice saw me in the front and told the crowd to give me a hand and the place went off – appreciation on command. It was a strange feeling. Before he said that, I had forgotten that there were all these people at the show in the first place. I was so much in my own world, it startled the hell out of me.

Worked out hard today. Did six interviews and met with BMG people. I can't remember their names but they were cool to me.

This morning was fucked. We drove last night from Chicago. I woke up in the parking lot of the gig less than two hours before I had to go on. I didn't even know where I was.

8.5.91 9:30 p.m., Cleveland OH Another good show. Same thing again, woke up in the parking lot of the gig and staggered around backstage trying to find out where the hell I was supposed to go. I must have looked like a damn fool. Finally someone led me to the dressing room. They gave us and the Butthole Surfers trailers in the back, near the mobile toilets. Nothing like being in the opening band.

Did a lot of interviews again, don't know how I pull them off. I don't remember what I say to these strangers.

I guess I did alright. Met more BMG people, they were alright. There sure are a lot of them.

I have a lot of body pain. Have been running a slight fever for two days now. I could barely stretch today. I guess I have some kind of cold. I thought I had it shook after the set was over but it's still with me. Tomorrow is a day off in Canada. We have a long drive tonight.

I feel alright besides the body ache. I am not lonely. I hold no thoughts, nor do they hold me. I am in the present. I have been reading about the code of the samurai. It has made me think about life differently. They were obsessed with death and had it on their minds all the time. It's one of the things that made them such fierce warriors. I have been able to use some of this to focus and stay hard. It has helped me with the loneliness that I have felt before on the road. I have had to find some way to deal with it because it is so ever present in my life. Even when I am with a woman, I am lonely. I have not figured that out yet but I'm working on it. To walk with death is to live eternities inside a moment. People seem different to me now. Their voices are nothing but a thick buzz of insects and the rustling of leaves.

Sometimes I imagine that people are dead when I talk to them. I don't remember the names. Their lives are meaningless, in piles. Sometimes when I look at them, I imagine killing them and eating while standing over their bodies.

The moron tech guy walks by me on his way to the back lounge of the bus. He has some stupid drunk woman with him. Shoot them both in the face and throw them into the parking lot. To live without morals, to be able to kill like Ted Bundy, that must be a strange strength. At the end of this, we're all dead. Insects.

8.6.91 8:57 p.m. Mississauga Canada Got here early in the morning. I hardly remember crossing into Canada. I slept a few hours and woke up in time to do five interviews that I wasn't told about. By the time they were all over, it was near six. Some day off.

The rest of the guys went into town to see a show. I am alone in the room listening to Alan Vega's new record. It's so good. He can't get a deal in the USA. I want to start a label badly. I would love to be able to put his records out here. There are some records that should really be out but are out of print. I would like to change this situation. I don't have the money to start a label but I want to. I know it would be a lot of work.

Wish this body ache would leave me. I don't know why my body does this to me. I think I tend to over-do it. Fuck it, I'll power through it like I always do.

10:32 p.m.: Just finished a call with Gail about starting the label. We have a meeting with Caroline on Monday. Keith isn't promising anything, but he did say he would meet with us. After that I faxed a letter to Alan Vega and his manager. I told them that I want to put out four records from his back catalog and listed all the things that I wanted to do with this label. I asked him to think about it and told that I would call him when I got stateside.

I don't remember today. It's late and I'm spaced out. Today was like being in a coma. I can't focus. Have a lot on my mind and it dulls me. I want to sleep without dreaming. I need to work, to keep busy, or else I'll cave in. I need to keep going forward or all is lost. I know that the line between pass and fail is a razor's width. I don't plan on blowing it.

8.7.91 10:45 p.m. Toronto Canada Played ok today. Took a while to get it going, sometimes it's hard to lose myself in the music. Spent the rest of the day walking around checking shit out. Did some interviews, that was not bad. Watched Ice-T, he was great as usual. A lot of people in my face for autographs, I wasn't up to it today. Sometimes I can't even get my mouth to open to talk to them. Sometimes I have to make it up as I go along. I don't feel anything in common with people a lot of the time and have to use sound bites to get by. They are cool to me but the things that they talk about have nothing to do with me. I have no idea what their world is like. They try to relate to me and I just don't get it.

After the show, I talked to Joey Ramone for a while. I have seen the Ramones play some great shows. It was so cool to hang out with him for a minute. He was a cool guy. When we played together in 1984, I never spoke to him.

So tonight, another drive, this time to Boston. I have a spoken show waiting for me there.

8.9.91 2:26 a.m. Boston MA Did the talking show tonight. Went well I think. I had a good time, the people were great. A lot of the folks from the tour showed up as well. Better than a night off any time. No good for going to Tower Records though. As we passed it, there was a fire engine outside and everyone was leaving. Just my luck, I show up and the damn place is burning down.

After the show tomorrow, I will leave with Mitch Bury of Adams, Mass and hit a gym. Looking forward to that. I think I'm hitting another exhaustion period. I flat out don't remember shit like I used to. I accidentally walked away from a guy that was talking to me tonight. I don't remember what he was talking about. On some of these days it's a good thing I keep a journal, otherwise I'd never remember what happened.

People must think I'm some kind of a waste case. All I know is that I've never had so many people in my face all the time like this ever in my life. I don't think I'm doing all that badly. Unless you were addicted to hype, how could you get used to all these people wanting to know every damn thing about you? Some days I don't even remember thinking. Maybe after we finish recording the next album, I should take some time to clear my mind of all the details and numbers that are filling it now. I don't even think of talking to women. Yesterday, the Ice-T posse kept coming over with messages from these girls who wanted to fuck me. I didn't even want to see them out of remote curiosity. After the show, I was changing up, getting ready to leave with Mitch Bury of Adams, Mass so we could go to the gym. One of the Syndicate boys came up to me and told me that this girl wanted to meet me. I didn't pay attention. This girl comes up to me and I forget exactly what she started out saying but she finished with, 'I want to suck your shorts dry!' I thanked her in my best narcotics agent imitation and flew out of there. Wanted to get to the gym. What a great line! Her enthusiasm was great. Next.

I am happy with my performance tonight. I am glad I was able to handle talking to them afterwards. The young ones mean a lot to me. I wouldn't want to bum them out by being too burnt out and twisted to be cool to them like they are to me. Sometimes I am not as nice as I would like to be. It's hard to be in a good mood all the time.

8.13.91 1:22 a.m. Albany NY Today was a day off. I went to New York after the show yesterday. Woke up this morning, called Alan Vega and checked in. Gail and I had a meeting with Keith at Caroline Records. We met with him to see if he was interested in putting out Alan's records. I played him some of Vega's stuff. Keith liked it a lot but was worried about how it would sell. I see why he might be hesitant, but I'm also tired of how labels are getting more conservative. I know the marketplace is tough but there has to be an effort to get out things that are truly great, even if they might not be able to sell a lot.

After that, I went to the airport and flew up here. Now at a hotel.

Other than that, I'm tired and sick of talking. I have interviews in the morning and then off to the gig. I'm more tired than I think. Right now, there's nothing I would like better than to be left alone, besides being able to play.

I know this girl that pulls the teasing trip on men. She used to do it with me, come to the show and be all into me and then all of a sudden, she would say she had to leave and she would be gone. I got together with her at one point. It was ok but I kept my distance. The other day, she came to the show even though I didn't put her on the list. She got backstage and talked to me. I ignored her for the most part. She did her 'I was just coming by to say hello' thing. All dressed up. What a joke. I said ok, bye and turned back to what I was doing. She came back a few minutes later and asked if she and her friend could get some kind of pass. I told her she was on her own and turned my back and that was it.

No more of the bullshit, less words. I can't stand talking to these women who play all this bullshit. They must hang out with guys who have no lives and will waste their time talking bullshit all night long. I don't want anything to do with them at all right now.

There is the playing and then there's death. Jazz music and the sword. I have been thinking about the girl I went out with last year. I learned a lot from her. I think it's better for me to keep my work in front of me and not let anything get in the way. This is the best thing for me. Sometimes I think women only rip your guts out if you let them in. I will not be stopped by a woman. I will never lose sleep over one of them again. That last time was pathetic. There's a last time for everything.

I will maintain myself even though I am exhausted and withdrawn. Death will guide me through. The Iron has been a tremendous help, the best thing I have ever found. I find strength in my body coming seemingly from nowhere now and it's telling me everything. Telling me that I'm right about the things that I'm doing and the course that I'm taking. I have been watching a lot of the others on this tour. Their bodies are weak and so are their minds. They have all this money and all these women around them and they have nothing at all. No drive, no hunger. The taste of blood isn't in their mouths and it shows. I have never been around so many musicians day-to-day like this. For the most part, they are a pretty weak bunch. There are some exceptions of course, but a lot of these people . . . I just don't get it. I think that rock musicians and actors are alike in a lot of ways.

8.14.91 1:35 a.m. Mt. Arlington NJ I didn't like the set today, I thought it was rushed and the people were dull to be in front of. It wasn't bad, but it never got what it needed.

Did the normal interview hustle after the set. After that, I had lunch. Ice-T came over with lyrics for 'There Goes The Neighborhood'. He and I are going to sing it tomorrow. I pretty much knew the words already but it's good having them there.

The rest of the day was spent left alone. I went out with Casey, Perry's wife, to do some video stuff out in the crowd. Just getting footage of people and talking to them and getting their take on the whole festival vibe. I learned a few things. I asked them if they were making new friends and everyone I asked said yes. That was interesting to me because I could never do that. I could never walk up to someone I didn't know and start talking to them, like what people do to me all the time.

I wouldn't want to meet people for the sake of meeting new people. It has never interested me. I think that maybe my view of people is a little skewed from the way I have interacted with them all these years. Since I was twenty, people have asked for my autograph. That kind of thing has made it hard to know what the difference is between fan, friend or enemy. If someone is a 'fan' of yours, can they be a friend? I am a fan of too many bands and musicians to mention and I guess I have some friends who are in bands that I like. Maybe that's ok because I'm in a band? I don't know. Joe Cole is my friend but I don't think he is a fan even though he likes the band. I guess there's no uniform rule to it. All I know is that when someone tells me that they have read everything I have written and have seen me play for many years, I am thankful but a little on-edge.

It was hard to walk around the more populated areas without having to do the autograph thing. It's not my idea of a good time. An intense girl gave me a drawing of me that I actually like. It's great – a black ink drawing of me with a gun in my mouth. It's liberally sprayed with her blood. She never smiled the whole time I spoke with her.

We drove here to NJ after Living Colour's set. Took a long time. We have to be up and at the venue in Stanhope in the morning. Man, this is a vacant brain I have right now. Too beat to think. I don't remember the van ride here very well even though I just got out. Mitch Bury of Adams, Mass came to the show today. I saw him and didn't want to talk to him at all. Not that I have any problem with him, it's just that I can't talk like I used to. I can't hang. With few exceptions, when I hear people talking, I want to get away. Time to sleep. Wish I had more to say in the journal. I read this back and it looks like a robot did it. Exhaustion has its teeth in me now.

One thing I have been noticing. This tour is hard to get away from. I get to the venue and see all the same people. I do the set, check out the Butthole Surfers and Ice-T, do the interviews and then food and workout. After that, I usually get on the bus, gel out and then walk around until Jane's Addiction goes on. I check them out and then we leave and drive all night. Wake up in the parking lot of the next venue and it starts all over again. I see nothing new. All these places look the same. It's really hard to remember where I am half the time.

8.15.91 11:53 p.m. Stanhope NJ Played well today. I liked it better than the show before. After our set, I had to do photos and interviews. I did a lot of them; I don't know how many. Talked to the girl from *Sassy* magazine, they're doing a feature on me in some upcoming issue. I did three or four photo sessions, I don't remember.

The best part of the day was playing with Body Count. I went up there for 'There Goes The Neighborhood' and ended up there for 'Voo Doo' and 'Cop Killer' as well. It was a blast. I don't think I blew out too badly.

The rest of the day was spent hanging out and doing chin-ups on the stage rigging. Talked to Morgan for a while. Watched Siouxsie and the Banshees play. After they walked off, the bass player went up and screamed at the bass tech because his monitors were feeding back. That's not her problem – he was a shithead; throwing his water, yelling like a child. He was hilarious in his make-up with his fat shaking all over. He looked like some strange woman. Right before Jane's Addiction went on, it started to rain like hell. I left because I could. I think the less time I spend there, the better. I got Thin Lizzy on the blaster, things are alright. There's not a lot to write about on this tour since we don't see that much. It's like living in a fish tank. There's only a week and a half left on the damn thing anyway. Seems like it's just started. It's been a good one as far as tours go.

Looks like in the morning, we'll have the green bus back. It went to Ohio with Dave, the driver, and got fixed. I heard that Dave had some experiences while he was waiting for the tow truck to come and take him to Ohio for the repair. First, a bogus tow truck tried to tow the bus away. The guy tried to tell Dave that he was legit. Then hours later, some kids tried to break into the hold below and he chased them off. All this on a highway. Some night.

The more I pull away from them, the more I like it. I don't need them to do my work. Sure it's great to have people at the shows and it's great that they get things out of what I do, but what they have to say to me has nothing to do with the work that I want to do. I can go the entire time after the interviews are over and not say anything to anyone and feel fine. I used to feel the need to make my point all the time. These days, fuck it, I have nothing to tell them that I didn't say when I was on stage. It's about that sword. I think of a samurai sword – its lean, spare beauty. There's no need for so much of the shit that comes out of people's mouths. I see how some people I'm around talk so much. One guy, it's as if he's addicted to talking to people. It's not for me. I have always admired the silent ones. Now I am someone that I can admire and respect. I think you can get to the point to where you see that there's no need to be right all the time and I think there's a point where you have seen enough that you can't talk about out loud. I think I'm getting to that point. I feel more at home with my writing than I do with talking to people. These days with all the interviews I'm doing, every time someone talks to me, it's one of those people. By the time I'm done with them, I have nothing to say to anyone.

8.15.91 8:01 p.m. McLean VA Today is a day off. We got the bus back this morning. We drove down here from New Jersey at around two. We're in the middle of nowhere. The hotel is having a convention for Japanese AmWay employees. The place is packed. So it's eight and the day off starts. I want to go into DC and check out Tower Records. The nearest Metro stop is a couple of miles away. I guess I'll take a cab. Better than the hotel room.

10:05 p.m.: Went to a Tower Records that happened to be across the highway. While I was in there, people came up and started talking to me. I felt myself getting pissed off but I fought it off. One guy sounded like he was on drugs, repeating the things I said as if thinking out loud. They wanted me to sign something and I told them I would as soon as I was finished being a customer. I got a Monk CD because it was on sale and split without signing anything. Walked up the highway and ate at a Wendy's. Yeah, that's the kind of shit we're in tonight. We have a 9:15 bus call in the morning. We play at noon.

Depression is here with me. I felt its hand on my shoulder as I walked against the traffic with my coffee in my hand. I should have kept walking. Every time depression hits me, I try to understand where it came from and why it's here. It's easier to deal with now that I know better than to try and talk to someone about it. That used to fuck me up badly, trying to explain myself, like talking to a girl as if that's going to do any good. What can anyone do for you in person? Records are better than real people. Empty rooms are better than fake talk and noise polluted time and space.

10:54 p.m.: Did some writing. Should try to get to sleep and wake up early. Too tired to workout. All I want to do is sleep without dreaming.

8.16.91 11:17 p.m. McLean VA Hanging out at the show, waiting to leave. Playing today was alright. A lot of people were there early so it was a full field of people. A lot of people were in my face today. I wasn't up to it. One of them was a very old friend of mine. Back in the day, he and I went through a lot together. Back then, he was always fucked up but it didn't bother me because he didn't get in my face. Today was different. He acted like a generic, drunk asshole. It hurt me to have to get away from him. It would have been so cool to have been able to talk to him, to see how he was doing. Seeing how fucked up he was, I guess it's not going well for him. Somehow people got backstage and were in my shit. Sometimes I can't even be halfway cool. I had to do a lot of interviews as well. Tonight we drive to North Carolina. Wake up at the venue and proceed.

Six more shows left on this tour. I am burned out on everything but playing. I am proud of myself that I have done over one hundred interviews. I reckon that's putting my time in.

8.17.91 8:27 p.m. Raleigh NC I thought we ripped shit up today. We played 'Blues Jam'. Felt good to get back to that one. I can't remember when we played it last, probably the other day. I'm so burnt that I wouldn't know. It's gotten to me in the last few days. I did one big interview with all these people at once today. That's the way we've been doing it the last few days so I don't have to hang out all day and answer the same questions over and over. One guy was trying to challenge me on all this shit, I run into punks like him all the time. He had no idea what he was dealing with until it was too late. It's funny when you get in their faces. They never expect you to be real.

I jammed with the Body Count boys today, same songs as the other time. It was better this time.

So now Siouxsie is on and I'm in the dressing room, I will retreat to the bus soon. Nothing is happening outside of the normal shit. The Butts got a shitty trailer outside so they came in here with us. Gibby got his 'Cam Ellman' wig and mustache on and went out. He brought back some young girls. Got in a good workout an hour ago. Nothing left to do now but wait to get out of here and get on to the next lonely station.

8.18.91 11:37 p.m. Atlanta GA Another good show today. We got in at some hour, I don't know. Another wakeup in the parking lot of the gig day situation. Got right to work, eating and stretching out. Hurt like hell. Played hard though, got a good sweat going even before I was on. After that I met with a lot of radio/store/BMG/Imago people. I didn't mind even though I don't remember any of their names and answered all their questions like I was asleep. After that I had to do interviews with nine journalist types. I was surrounded by tape recorders. I did the best I could. After that I waited for forty minutes to do a video interview. They were too late for me to hang out any more so I left. I went out into the plaza and watched this performance guy named Deacon Lunchbox. He was great, he's on the *Alive From Off Center* show that I was on for PBS. Later on, I watched Jane's Addiction. They were good but not as good as the last few nights. Perry was talking a lot about Moses. It was strange and hard to follow at times. After their set, all the bands and crew went outside and did a group photo. MCA made us all sweatshirts with Lollapalooza logos on them and congratulated us on being on the biggest tour of 1991. Hell, we outdrew Van Halen at the gig today. Whoa.

In a while we leave to drive to Orlando FL. It's a day off. I'd rather play but my body could use a rest. Another night in the fish tank. It will be strange being off this tour. I think of the fact that I'll be home next week for a few days. The tour will be over and it will be fall. I was thinking of this today. It's like summer camp coming to an end. I will miss this for a while at least. I try my best not to let anything matter, not to attach to anything or anyone.

8.19.91 1:36 p.m. Orlando FL Day off today. Got in around 9:30 a.m. Slept for a while. I'm in a clean room and Alan Vega is on the blaster. Feeling pretty lifeless, waiting for the coffee to kick in. No interviews today. Don't know what I'll do with myself. Listen to how boring I am, like a robot. Disconnected. Don't tell anyone I'm pathetic.

I thought I would never play in Orlando again. After the bullshit that went down on the last Black Flag show in '86, no way. That was a hell of a night with all the skinheads surrounding the mixing board, the Cuban bouncers wanting to stab them. I will make sure to talk about some of that shit tomorrow.

6:29 p.m.: What a depressing place. Went to this mall across the highway. Most of the stores are closed, people sit in their cars and drink. Depressed and staggering America, bloated and dying – I see it clearly when I come to places like this. Lots of room but no one can afford to live here. Orlando is a good place to go to if you want to get bummed out enough to kill yourself. Fuck it.

8.21.91 12:10 a.m. Orlando FL We got to the gig at 10 a.m. today. It was raining and the crew was bumming out. They were jamming, trying to get the production on according to schedule.

When we went on, it was raining but we still kicked it. I told the crowd why I never wanted to come to Orlando again. I told them that I thought the skinheads should be taken out into the street and shot in the head. Skins started seig heiling me and flipping me off. The crowd made one hell of a noise and the skins bummed. I said a bunch of other shit but I forget it now.

After the set, I had to meet with some radio and BMG/Imago people. Made it out of there in time to sing with Ice-T. After that, it was lunch and a few interviews. I talked with Dion, the guy who did 'Runaround Sue'. I have a couple of Dion and the Belmonts records. He's friends with the owner of the place and his daughter is a fan of Jane's Addiction. I took a photo with him. He was really cool. He told me he dug what I was saying to the skinheads during the set. He told me about being on tour in the 50s down south with Sam Cooke and how he had to go into restaurants and get him food because Sam couldn't go in because he was black. He said something that was great. He said that he did all things out of pride and never out of fear. He never knew about racism until he went down south. He said he was from Brooklyn and people were just people. He talked about hanging out with James Brown at the Apollo. He said that he did his tours with a black band and when he got the chance to be in a movie with his music, they made him use an all-white band. I learned a lot. He was great to talk to, I'll never forget it.

I am sick of racism. It takes all the fun out of things in this country. It made my life growing up in DC a living hell. I was always running from the black boys who wanted to beat my ass for no good reason. The irony that stands out to me is that we liked the same music. I wonder if we connected on that level, would there have been any of that nonsense in the first place.

Later on in the day, I did this video with Ice. We talked about freedom and racism for about forty-five minutes. We sat in the back of the NIN bus and kicked it in front of a video 8 cam. I have learned a lot from Ice-T.

Some shit happened earlier in the day. Some skins beat up some people in the crowd. One skin hit some dude with a bottle. Steve from Jane's Addiction got it all on video. The pigs came and nailed the skins but the kid that got the bottle is afraid to press charges because he knows that they will kick his ass or worse. They would. I don't blame the guy but it's how these assholes get away with all this shit.

Watched Jane's Addiction tonight, they were good – better than the other night in Atlanta. Other than that, that's the day. I fly to Miami in the morning, tomorrow night I do a talking show there. Better than a night off. Looks like I will also do a talking show on one of the days off in Seattle. I feel good, four more shows to go. Looking forward to heading west.

We lost NIN tonight, glad of it. Tired of listening to that bullshit everyday. The road crew was hard to take. Nice enough people but they were getting shit on so much by Trent that they were all nervous wrecks, all afraid of losing their jobs. Every night all the busted equipment was on the floor of the bus as they scrambled to fix it for the next day's show. I asked them why the band wrecked their shit all the time. I was told that it's part of the act. Before the show, they tell Trent what he can break and what he can't, according to what is fixed and what they have backups of. So it's all choreographed. I remember one day we had to leave from a hotel extra early so we could drive into a town and get corn starch for the band to put on their faces for their make-up. How weak is that? I have to lose sleep because some guy needs fucking corn starch to put on his face. Please. I can't remember where we were but we were on the bus late at night and the sound guy, the main ass kisser in the crew, started telling us all about how the band filled up the toilet with their shit and didn't flush it so the cleanup person would have a nice little surprise. All I could think of is someone with an already shitty job walking into that. I said I thought that was pretty weak and the sound guy went off on me.

'HEY, GET OFF TRENT'S BACK, MAN!'

Uh, ok. I guess it is cool when overpaid rockstars can leave shit for people to clean up. I can't wait to do it tomorrow!

I just sat and let this fool talk. I was so proud of myself for not breaking his nose. It would have been too easy.

8.22.91 9:46 p.m. Dallas TX Played well today. Not many people at the show but it didn't matter, we had a good time anyway. Flew in from Miami ok, didn't get much sleep though.

Today we picked up Fishbone. They were cool when they played. Angelo, the singer guy, walks around with his horn and plays it in your room like it's the only thing you want to hear. Now it's in the room next door doing it and it's hard to take. He should get his own TV show. He's a good guy though. Great band. I don't like being around musicians, too much like actors. I can't understand people backstage. It seems like all they do when they're not onstage is hang out, drink and talk a bunch of shit. The Butts and their friends came in and polished off most of our beer. No problems there. I don't drink the shit but it would be nice if they could ask instead of acting like it was theirs. I don't care. That's one of the problems I see on

LOLLAPALOOZA TOUR JOURNAL

tours like this one. Little things get to be big things. When you live in this little world, your values adhere to the environment you're in. This environment is so much bullshit. I like the playing part and that's it. The rest is the rest.

We play here tomorrow but we don't have to be there until noon so I'll be able to get some sleep. I want to stay and see Jane's Addiction but the racket is getting to me. I have come to the point where I can't even take people saying hello to me. Today there were these two boys by the back gate. I was sitting alone and they kept waving at me. I waved back at them and thought nothing more of it. One of them held up a record of mine. Yeah, so you have a record. I leave and come back after lunch and they're still there waving. I walk over to the gate and ask them what the fuck they want. They want me to sign pictures from the Gap thing and the record. They stayed there for over ninety minutes waiting to maybe talk to me. I laid into them, telling them that they shouldn't waste their lives waiting for people to sign their pieces of paper. You would think that they would have a life of their own. I signed the shit. What else am I going to do? I can't respect that shit. How can people lower themselves like that. I can see people doing that kind of shit for Van Hagar. The people that are into them should stand for hours in the hot sun and get dissed. I would hope people that are into me would hate themselves for lowering themselves to that begging shit. Fuck it, act like a fucking man.

8.24.91 12:31 a.m. Dallas TX Had a good time playing today, the Surfers came out and finished it with us. It was a good jam. Today there was a sellout crowd so a lot of people were there when we played. I don't know if they liked us or not, that kind of shit never occurs to me. Had a good time throwing the radio guy offstage. They always have some local DJ that's sponsoring the gig come out right before we go out and hype the people up. This one wouldn't get off stage so I bulldozed his ass off.

I sang three songs with Body Count as well. That was a blast. I'll miss those guys.

Later on in the evening, this shithead that looks just like the other shithead Al Jorgensen, wants to talk to me about Al. Seems like Al bummed on the way I treated him in Chicago. I told the fuck just what I told Al. This one told me about how tough it was to watch his fellow junkie friends die right in front of them. What the fuck did they think was going to happen? Anyway the guy looked just like Al — used, dead with stupid hair. I hope they die together. On a better note, Jane's Addiction was fucking amazing tonight. I think they are one of best live rock bands there ever was. When they're on, there's nothing like it in the world.

There's not much to write about with the way things are. The days pass with regularity. The halls all look the same and day after day I see the same faces. The Violent Femmes played today. They were great. They play on the last two shows. Fuck, two shows left. Watching Jane's Addiction tonight really made me feel it. It's like we're some kind of big gang but it's not. When you think that you have someone behind you, someone in your corner, that's when you find out you don't. I have plane tickets to leave a few hours after our set on the 28th. I will be in the air or in my room when Jane's Addiction are playing. The thought of that fucks with me a bit. Makes me want to stay for the last set and see it come to an end. I don't like the idea that there could be music playing while I'm home. On the other hand, it's not like it's my set and it's not good to attach to shit. All those good-byes would suck as well. Maybe it's good to just slip out of there and disappear. I don't know, I think it's better to get out of there and get with the idea that it's over. Hanging around is just living a lie, wanting it not to be over and trying to feel better about it by hanging around like a sucker. I remember this feeling before, when I did this UCLA student film and there was the wrap party. It was a drag because we were all bummed out that we had to leave each other after working so closely. It was good to get on to other things though.

We have to get up early in the morning and fly to Denver. It's a day off for us. My feet are swollen and aching. I think the concrete stages are hard on them. They hurt all the time now.

8.27.91 2:28 p.m. Denver CO At the hotel, in the middle of nowhere near a small plane airport. At least there's a good gym here. Day off in the middle of nowhere. Nothing to do, I don't think we're too close to the city.

4:24 p.m.: We really are in the middle of nowhere. It's like some strange industrial block. Body is sore but I'm still going to go for the workout. I talked to Don today. He and Selby are going to the festival in Holland. They have to stay a week to make the ticket work, apparently it's not a problem. I'm exhausted. I have nothing on my mind. I can stare at the wall for an hour and not notice.

We play tomorrow at noon. Have to get up early. I have a lot of business stress on my mind – book company stuff.

I figured if you're cool to everybody that works with you, they will be cool back. From dealing with the band, I see that it's not always true. I am filled with confusion and tension. I have to keep it to myself and keep myself together. Sometimes it's more than I can take but I do it and will continue to. As if anyone was ever going to stop me, what a joke.

8.25.91 10:50 p.m. Denver CO The set went ok today. Had some problems with the lack of rich air but I made it through ok. Vernon Reid jammed with us on 'Move Right In'. He ripped it up. After that I met the usual people and talked for a while. I wasn't good with the people today. The backstage was located near the crowd so they could just look in and call to you. There was really nowhere to go without being seen. Not a good day for dealing with people. I don't get along with people anymore – it all seems antagonistic. I can't find any patience within myself. I got letters from girls today. I read them and they made me mad. I don't know why. I think it's because no one knows the reasons why I do what I do and when they compliment me, it makes me furious.

8.26.91 6:22 p.m. Auburn WA Just got here. Day off today. The hotel is in the middle of nowhere again, twenty miles from Seattle, fifteen miles from the venue. Spent most of the day on airplanes. Will go into the city in a while.

I'm tired and withdrawn, don't want to talk to anyone. That's the way it is for me now. I need to get away from people. I can't take the questions anymore, voices on the phone, people who want to talk to me. It all makes me sick. The room is good.

8.27.91 12:48 a.m. Auburn WA Did a talking show tonight. Night off for the band. Hardly anyone there but still it was a good one. The hall and the audience were great. Better than a night off any time. Walked around a lot today, hit some record stores and got stuff for the guys. After tours I like to try to give them all something, the last time it was CDs. I'd like to give them money, like a bonus, but there isn't the money to do that. Someday though.

Got recognized a lot today, got hard to take after a while. I wear down. Getting stared at in the record store made me feel fucked up. I just got back from Denny's – the place was full of people who stared and pointed throughout the meal. Whatever.

Back at the hotel, the next journal entry will probably be post-tour. Sad to see this one end but it will be good to get away from it. This is a good tour but it's not reality for me. I couldn't tour like this year round. I see this kind of thing making bands break up and play really shitty. I am exhausted again. I don't have a lot of stamina right now, I think it's just burnout. Time to pull it in.

8.28.91 11:33 p.m. LA CA I'm back in my room. I did the set hours ago. We played ok, it was a last-show-of-the-tour type show for me. I fall into that shit from time to time. At one point, someone threw a shoe at me. Right after that, someone spat at me. I usually don't give a fuck about shit like that, but today it got to me. I told the crowd that next time they want to spit, they should come up real close and do it in my face and I'll take my turn. Fuck these people, throwing shit. It was raining when we played. After we finished, it got worse, got colder. While the next band played, steam came from the pit. We did a photo session for *Rip* magazine. I did this interview with some kid. He was asking the 'idiot with no respect for your time' questions. 'When you piss, do you aim for the water or the back of the bowl?' Shit like that just makes me want to smack the guy for an answer. I can usually keep myself together. Today, it was impossible. I told the guy that if he asked more bitch questions, I was out of there. He had only a few questions after that. At that point, I had all I could take of the Lolla bullshit. Luckily for me, I left soon after. Before I left, someone was talking about the band No Means No and their shirt that makes fun of my back tattoo. I said that I wanted to get my cut. Our bass player said that it was a parody and that I couldn't get anything from it. Of course I wasn't talking about any legal shit. I was talking about fucking their shit up when I run into them. The bass player said that I should just take it as a joke and relax. At that moment I had the overwhelming urge to smack him like the bitch that he is. Not that he would ever be able to handle anyone doing anything to him – he'd shit his pants. I don't look forward to working with him on this album. He's such a weak piece of shit.

So I got out of there and it felt great. I'm sick of people recognizing me and I'm sick of answering questions. I flew back and when I got out in front of my place, the driver started giving me shit, telling me to hurry up and get my money out. I am proud of myself, I didn't do anything. I gave him his money and he took off. I was setting up the punch. I was losing control. I could feel it. That shithead will never know how close he came to getting fucked up.

Good to be in my room. There were twelve messages on my machine. Good for me that I took the tape out when I left after the Irvine shows. There's nothing for me to listen to. I got some James Brown playing and I'm starting to cool down. All I can think of is belting that cab driver.

The guys in the band insist that they get paid for the few days that we are practicing. We had set up a flat fee for everybody that included the pre-production. Now it seems that it doesn't. I said sure, pay them, make them happy. Hired hands, that's all they are to me. I think I'll do one set of band pictures and then from then on, it's just pictures of me. Hired hands, fine. I'll treat them just like hired hands.

Good to be here. I don't want to talk to anyone. I want the world to leave me alone.

THE IRON

I believe that one defines oneself by re-invention To not be like your parents. To not be like your friends. To be yourself. To cut yourself out of stone.

When I was young, I had no sense of myself. I was a product of all the taunts and threats at school combined with the fear and humiliation I dealt with on a regular basis. At school I was told that I would never amount to anything. One 'instructor' as they were called, took to calling me 'garbage can' in front of the other students. I could never talk back to an instructor so I had to sit still and take it. I started to believe them after a while. I was skinny and spastic. When others would tease me, I didn't run home crying and wondering why. I knew very well why they antagonized me. I was that which was there to be antagonized. In sports, I was laughed at and never chosen to be on a team. I was pretty good at boxing but only because the rage that filled my every waking moment made me wild and unpredictable. I fought with a strange fury. The others thought I was crazy. I was not respected, just observed to see what I would do next.

I hated myself. As stupid as it seems now, I wanted to be like my fellow students in every way. I wanted to talk like them, dress like them, carry myself with the ease that one does when he knows he's not going to get pounded in the hallway between classes. When I looked in the mirror and saw my sallow face staring back, I wanted nothing more than to be transformed into one of them, just for a night to see what it would be like to have some of their seemingly well adjusted happiness.

Years passed and I learned to keep it all inside. I would only talk to a certain few of the boys in my grade that were losers like me. To this day, some of those guys are some of the coolest people I've ever known. You hang out with a guy that's gotten his head pushed into a toilet a few times and you treat him like you would want to be treated, you'll have a good friend there. Some of these guys were so funny. They saw things that the better looking, more well groomed members of our school would never see, knew things they would never know. I believe that they were the better for it. They definitely had the best jokes.

I had an instructor in history. His name was Mr. Pepperman. I am forever in his debt. Mr. Pepperman commanded intense respect and fear all over the school. He was an absolutely no bullshit, powerfully built Viet Vet who barely spoke outside of class. No one talked out of turn in his class except once that I can remember. It was the class president. Mr. Pepperman lifted the boy off the ground by the lapels of his jacket and pinned him to the blackboard. That was it, as far as talking out of turn in class, or being late either.

One day in October, Mr. Pepperman asked me if I had ever worked out with weights. Actually he said something like, 'You're a skinny little faggot. This weekend, have your mommy take you to Sears and buy one of those one hundred pound sand-filled weight sets and drag it home. I'll show you how to use it.'

This was encouraging. He was not the nicest person I have ever met in my life but at least he cared enough to tell me that much.

Since it was Mr. Pepperman telling me to do this, I did it. I figured he would throw me across the room if I didn't. I got the weights into the basement somehow and left them on the floor. I was looking forward to Monday with a strange anticipation which I had never felt before in my short life. He had told me to buy the weights and I had done it. Something was sure to happen.

Monday came. I was called into his room after school. He asked if I had bought the weights. I told him that I had. What he told me next was something I'll never forget. He said that he was going to show me proper ways to lift weights. He was going to put me on a program and he was going to start hitting me in the solar plexus in the hallway when I wasn't looking. When I could take the punch, then I would know that I was getting somewhere. At no time was I to look at myself in the mirror to see signs of change nor was I to tell anyone at school what I was doing. I promised. I was going to make a list of all the reps and the weights I was lifting at so I could monitor my progress, if I managed to make any. I was to turn in the chart at Christmas break. Never had anyone given me that much encouragement. He told me that it was going to be hard but I would like it if I gave it my all.

I went home that night and started right in on the exercises he had taught me. It was hard finding what weight was right for each lift but I soon fell into step.

I never missed a single workout. Sometimes I would do the workout twice. Immediately I noticed that my appetite grew incredibly. I was eating at least twice what I usually did. It felt like I could not get enough food into me. When I would visit my father on the weekends, he started calling me 'the locust'.

Weeks passed and every once in a while Mr. Pepperman would give me a shot and drop me in the hallway sending my books all over the place. The other students didn't know what to think. All the while I had this great secret that I wasn't telling anyone. I hadn't looked at myself in the mirror. I did everything he told me to do down to the letter. As the weeks went by, I steadily added more weight to the bar. I could feel the power inside my body grow.

Exams came right before Christmas break. I was walking to class and from out of nowhere Mr. Pepperman appeared and gave me a shot in the chest. I laughed and kept walking. That afternoon Mr. Pepperman told me to bring in the chart the next day. I was still not allowed to look at myself or tell anyone of my secret work. I brought in the chart and he looked it over and asked if I had really come that far. I told him yes and I was proud of myself and I never felt like this in my life. He said that I could go home and look at myself now.

I got home and ran to the bathroom and pulled my shirt off. I could not recognize myself at first. My body had a shape. It was a body, not just this thing that housed a stomach and a heart. I could see the difference big time. It was the first thing that I remember ever giving me a sense of accomplishment. I felt and looked strong. I had done something. No one could ever take it away. You couldn't say *shit* to me.

It took me years to fully appreciate the value of the lessons learned from the Iron. It wasn't until my late twenties that I learned that I had given a great gift to myself. I had learned to apply myself and that nothing good came without work and a certain amount of pain. You can kick ass in anything you want to do when you apply yourself completely. To this day, all the lessons I learned when I was fifteen are still with me.

I used to think that the Iron was my enemy and I was trying to lift that which did not want to be lifted. My triumph was making the Iron do what I wanted it to do, the thing that it did not want to do – move. I see now that I was wrong. When the Iron doesn't want to come off the hooks, it's the kindest thing it can do for you. It's trying to help you. If it flew up and went through the ceiling, then it wouldn't be doing you any good. It's not resisting you in the least. That's the way the Iron talks to you. My triumph is to work *with* the Iron. The material you work with is that which you will come to resemble. That which you work against will always work against you, including yourself.

I used to fight the pain through the workout. My triumph was to take it and bear it all the way through. Hating the pain and the way it made me feel. Recently the lesson was made clear to me. The pain that fills my body when I hit it is not my enemy. It is the call to greatness. It's my body trying to pull me higher.

People usually go so far. Pain keeps them back. There is pain on many different levels. To change is painful. To go after something that's out of your reach is painful. Pain doesn't have to be a deterrent. Pain can inspire you to reach past yourself. When dealing with the Iron, one must be careful to correctly interpret the pain. You must seek proper instruction so you don't injure yourself. Most injuries involved with the Iron come from ego. Try to lift what you're not ready for and the Iron will teach you a lesson in restraint and self-control. I once spent a few weeks lifting weight that my body wasn't ready for and spent a few months of not picking up anything heavier than a fork. It was my ego that made me try to lift weight that was still several months and workouts away.

Through the years, I have combined meditation, action, and the Iron into a single strength. Only when the body is strong can the mind think strong thoughts. It's up to an individual's character what he does with this strength. The difference between a big bouncer who gets off strong-arming people and putting them in pain and Mr. Pepper-man and his gift of strength.

The strength I have attained through the combined efforts of what I described earlier is a One Relationship. The mind and body develop strength and grow as a single thing. Go out and see for yourself. The strongest number is One. Aspire to the One and understand strength and balance.

I cannot believe a weak person who says they have true self-respect. I have never met a truly strong person that didn't have it. I think that a lot of inwardly and outwardly directed contempt passes itself off for self-respect.

I have found that the Iron is a great cure for loneliness. Loneliness is a desire for what is not there with you. You can be lonely for an infinite number of things – people, feelings – whatever creates a void in your life with its absence. Sometimes your loneliness has nothing to attach itself to. You're just lonely, flat out. The Iron can pull you through when all else fails. You'll find that it was you that got you through. Loneliness is energy, powerful as hell. People kill themselves sick on loneliness. They drink themselves into the floorboards. They do all kinds of damaging things to themselves to combat their loneliness. The loneliness is real. The energy is real. I can't see what good it does to damage yourself trying to feel better. If one can apply all this real energy to damaging oneself, then isn't it possible to harness all this energy into something positive to combat loneliness?

Time spent away from the Iron makes my mind and body degenerate. I turn on myself and wallow in thick depression that makes me unable to function. The body shuts my mind down. The Iron is the best anti-depressant I have ever found. No better way to fight weakness than with strength. Fight degeneration with generation. Once the mind and body have been awakened to their true potential, there is in many ways, no way to turn back. You might not remember when you started working out but you'll remember when you stopped and you won't look back at it with much joy because you know you're depriving yourself of yourself.

The Iron will always kick you the real deal. You work out correctly and patiently and maintain a good diet and you will become stronger. You don't work out for a while and muscle will go away. You get what you put into it. You learn the process of becoming.

Life is capable of driving you out of your mind. The way it all comes down these days, it's some kind of miracle if you're not insane. People have become separated from their bodies. I see them move from their offices to their cars and on to their homes. They stress out constantly. They lose sleep. Their egos run wild. They become motivated by that which will eventually give them a massive stroke. You never have to lose it. You really don't. There's no excuse for freaking out at the workplace, school, anywhere. No need for a mid-life crisis. You need the iron mind.

The Iron is always there for you. Your friends may come and go. Someone you thought you knew might turn out to be someone you can no longer stand to be around in the time it takes to blink your eye. Fads come and go, almost everything comes and goes. However, the Iron is the Iron. Two hundred pounds is always two hundred pounds. The Iron is the great reference point, the all-knowing perspective giver, always there like a beacon in pitch black. I have found the Iron to be my greatest friend. It never freaks out on me, never runs, never lies.

Originally appeared in DETAILS

RANDOM BAD ATTITUDE

It's hard to get along with people As much as you try to like them and accept them as individuals, it becomes difficult because they keep getting out of line and wasting your time. All it takes is one of these people a day dumping their weakness at your feet and for the rest of the day, you feel the need to kill all of them.

The other day, I was in Hamburg, Germany walking to a bank to change some of the Queen's cash for some of those sturdy German marks. I was looking at the display in the window of a store. The only things in the window were knives, guns and sticks for pigs, like the ones the steroid-driven bastards used on good ol' Rodney King. A man walks up to me and gets in my face and starts giving me a load of shit. I guess there was something about me that he didn't like, or maybe he was a typical piece of human garbage and was trying to communicate. No matter, the only thing that occurred to me was to go into the store and get one of those Rambo III knives that were in the window and stab this air-taking, dung-producing, waster-of-my-time in his neck. Needless to say it took me a while to get back to my normal fun-loving, people-liking self.

I try to be a good guy, but it seems I keep getting set back all the time. Last night, I was doing a talking show in Berlin. I was talking about what it was like to hear the report of the handgun that shot the brains out of my best friend's head and left him in the fetal position on the front walk of 809 Brooks Ave. in Venice, California on 12.19.91.

Some guy starts yelling at me, the only thing I could make out was, 'Get real baby!' I guess that homicide isn't real enough. Maybe I should have gotten off the stage and bit him in the face and given him some of the germs that I've got and then he would start having the same symptoms that I have and I wouldn't have to feel so alone. Maybe this guy would have called me up in the middle of the night and told me that he has the classic symptoms of the blues – a good man feeling bad. The rest of the night was a turn-off. So much for Berlin.

The only way I have found to deal with the urban contemporary reality that I find myself in has been to go unplugged. I have unplugged myself from much of the arteries of music and culture. I've seen and heard enough crap, dodged enough bullets, threats and seen enough vulgar displays of power to last me the rest of my days. Instead of getting frustrated at the fact that I can rarely go to the record store and go to the new release rack and buy something that I can get into, I just stopped going. Why is there so much meaningless, waste of time music out there these days? I'm no snob. I know I'm right about this. You can sell a lot of people a lot of crap but you can't sell it to me. Finding a good band to listen to these days is harder than ever. When one comes along, it's such a surprise when it didn't used to be. It's a surprise I could use a lot more of.

Some of the bullshit that they foist on you every day. You know when you see the CD single a band releases, you'll see one of the album tracks and then some lame edit (like you really care about the shortened version that they used to make the video), and an unreleased track. You buy it wanting to hear the extra song that you didn't get on the album that was only about forty-five minutes anyway. In your mind you know that CDs can take up to eighty minutes of information. They could of let you have the extra song from the beginning but they see it fit to milk you one more time. But hey, you're a fan so you buy the CD and you play it and the song is ok. A week later, you see another version of the single – it's the single track with yet another unreleased song. To get all the music from the band's new recording sessions, you must shell out more money to hear another few minutes of music. Not the kind of thing I would do to anyone that would be kind enough to part with their money to hear something that I have done. Why do they do that mean stuff to the fans? So the record company can put the single into the charts so the song will show up on the right list and the guy can tell his boss that the band has a single in the charts. You pay for every step. Sounds like you're getting taken for a ride to me. Have a nice choke. I won't be there to hear you gag, I figure you deserve anything that happens to you for hanging out with the beast. The record company tried to play that bullshit with me several months ago and after repeating the word 'no' to the guy several times he got it into his skull that I wasn't with it. It's easy to be fooled by Bono. He talks a good game. He's a good con but he shows his colors too often. The good con artist knows how to play the mark and not give anything away. That's where good old bubblebutt blows it. If he played that shit in my neighborhood, the local crack dealers would have taken him out a long time ago.

I'm not into censoring bands or getting in their way or dragging them down. The Ledge has the right to rock as much as you and I do, but excuse me if I don't show up for the gig, I'd rather watch paint dry. It's hard to watch fake bands get away with the crimes that they do. They take your good intentions and goodwill and turn it against you. It's like pushing a guy in a wheelchair onto the motorway.

There's a lot of good music in places where you might never thought to have searched. Cab Calloway, Fats Waller, Duke Ellington, Charlie Parker, Coltrane, Miles, Sun Ra, Robert Johnson, etc. Check out some guys who played and didn't have MTV to care about. People who played music because it was their lives, not some career move. Thelonious Monk didn't hire songwriters to come in and give his career a lift; he played the piano and died and that's it. It's people like the ones I just listed that show out so many of the contemporary types for exactly what they are – lazy posers with no courage and no soul.

Modern record companies couldn't handle someone like Miles Davis who turned out two to four albums a year. Major labels these days wouldn't know what to do with a lifeforce like that. They would be totally over-whelmed and probably tell Miles that it would be a better business move if he wasn't so productive. Better to spend a year making ten songs in the studio and release bullshit money draining remixes of the ten songs for the next two years while you go out and 'promote' the ten songs. What a way to go through life, with a wimper instead of a roar. It happens all the time. Never forget whom you're living for. Don't let any of these bastards take you to the cleaners. How do you know I'm not one of them? Here's why: I don't give a flying fuck what you think of me.

I hope all of you live a long time and find some meaning in the middle of all the bullshit and the bullets.

Originally appeared in NEW MUSICAL EXPRESS

ROKY ERICKSON

Getting to work with Roky Erickson is an honor I own the company that publishes his fine collection of lyrics, *Openers II.*

Last summer I was able to meet the man and some of his family. I have never met anyone remotely like Roky. Never heard music like his anywhere else either.

The people around Roky are very protective. The entire list of circumstances that led to Roky's current state are elusive and wrapped in rumor, legend and double talk.

The man himself is at once fascinating, enigmatic, frustrating, charming, and unlike anyone you will ever encounter. When you're with him, you're in his world, on his time and that's all there is to it.

And then there's the music. Those who know, *know.* They get it, believe it and will go to great lengths to hear more. Roky is easily one of the greatest figures in American music, period. There are many instances when nothing will hit the spot but a 13th Floor Elevators or a Roky record. His piercing vocal is soulfully chilling and unforgettable. Even upon first listen, he grabs you immediately.

I have been a fan ever since I heard the Elevators in 1981. Imagine the high it was to get a call at the company from one Casey Monahan, asking if we would be interested in publishing the official collection of Roky's lyrics, *Openers II.* I don't think we have so readily said yes to a project ever.

It was at this time that I was to be pulled into the orbit around Planet Erickson. Casey told me how it was with

Roky and what was going on with the tangle of publishing rights for his music and the frustration he was dealing with, going toe-to-toe with these bastards who seemed bent on ripping off Roky until he was dead and gone.

Casey sent a rough manuscript to us and we were more than impressed. Besides the greatness of the lyrics was the work that Casey had put in on his own time. Casey has a very full-time job and was doing this because of his love for Roky and the music that he has given us. A hell of a lot of energy given to a guy who refused to help with the book and often didn't acknowledge that it was in the works at all. I was later to find out that many who surround Roky give their time and effort generously. I became one.

As the months went by, Casey was finding more songs in notebooks, warehouses, via fax and off video tapes of performances. The incoming sets of lyrics seemed to be endless.

I flew to Austin on July 14, 1994 to meet Roky and Casey. I met Roky at his birthday celebration. That night I was to meet one of his brothers, his son and some of the people who surround him. Below are my notes from the visit.

7.14.94 Austin TX: Met Roky Erickson. Asked if my tattoos were strings holding me up. He asked Casey if I was his bodyguard. He told some guy that he had 'Donald Duck playing ukulele.' He wandered out and sang some songs with the band that was onstage celebrating his birthday, 'You're Gonna Miss Me', 'Don't Slander Me', 'Two Headed Dog' and 'Starry Eyes'. I met his son Jegar and his brother Sumner.

7.15.94 Austin TX: Hung out with Roky for several hours. He signed the contract for the lyric book. Roky is a one-line artist. It's all good too. In the lawyer's office, 'We're way up here in hell!' He motions to all the people around him and asks no one in particular, 'Are we going to keep these slaves around?' Asked his brother Sumner, 'Where did you get all that hair? Did you get sick or something?' About the money from the signing, 'It's ok? It gives us food stamps?' When he couldn't smoke in the room he put the cigarette back in the pack and said, 'It's like Houdini!'

Later on I went to his place. About ten radios were on in different rooms. I counted about 5–7 televisions on – Roky's 'Electronic Friends'. Piles of mail order stuff everywhere. I could barely speak over the din. The septic tank had broken under his place and a corner of his little bedroom stank and the floor was wet. He pointed at the chair that was in the corner and said, 'I think there's some rats under there.' It was fascinating and depressing. I took Casey's camera and took some pictures of the rooms and the front of his house.

Went to Casey's and watched Roky footage on video. Watched him synch 'You're Gonna Miss Me' on *American Bandstand* back in the 60s. To see his face then, so sharp and handsome, and then to think about him in that fucked up place with all the noise twenty-four hours a day made me feel exhausted. I went through one of his notebooks. Lyrics on one side and logarithmic math work going down the other.

Later on, a local cable show showed half an hour of live footage of Roky playing as well as some footage of him with his son. At the end of the show the screen flashed 'Happy Birthday, Roky'. It made me cry.

Months went by and numerous versions of the book went back and forth through the mail. Songs kept coming in and Sumner and Casey kept finding changes and errors. I spent a week going through the book myself, reading through sets of lyrics while listening to the songs on the stereo. Sometimes the words were hard to understand and the fact that Roky uses very unique phrasing and sentence structure didn't help things go quickly either.

I think besides the sheer power of Roky's music, the most amazing thing about Roky is the love that surrounds him. All these people who have put in time above and beyond the call of duty like Casey and the guys over at Trance who put out Roky's new record, the people in the club the night of his birthday party, all the people who said hello to him when we walked down the street or went into a restaurant. It was beyond words. And in the middle was Roky with his arms crossed with that beaming and slightly amused look on his face. I know he gets it. I think he knows how lucky he is.

Originally appeared in THORAZINE

THE DEVIL'S MUSIC

I was asked by Elektra Records to interview Jerry Lee Lewis for his video press kit that was to correspond with his new album *Young Blood* The label thought it would be interesting to have the both of us in the same frame. I accepted the job. I have been a fan of 'The Killer' for many years and I figured it would be an experience if nothing else.

The deal was that I was to go to Memphis and drive into Mississippi where Jerry Lee lives and interview him at the Lewis ranch.

I dove back into my complete Sun recordings of Lewis – an eight CD set with all of the outtakes and master takes. It had been a while since I had heard it and wanted to see if it sparked anything that would be worth asking him.

I read anything I could find on Jerry Lee Lewis. Hell of a story from all the different accounts. Quick rise to fame and quick fall out. The history on that is well documented so I won't bother to recap it here.

Night after night I listened to the CDs. The genius is overwhelming, scary. During the takes before the master, you can hear him approaching the ultimate version and then it happens and it is truly startling. There's something about his voice and his piano playing on the Sun recordings that is pure evil – real devil's music. It made me wonder how I was going to handle meeting him thinking about all the things I had heard about his violent temper. As well, I had been playing an advance tape of *Young Blood* and was surprised at its power. His playing is strong as ever and the vocals are fine. It's a good record.

On March 30, 1995, I was on a plane from LA to Memphis. I got to the hotel in the late afternoon. A few hours later I met up with two people from Elektra and Jerry Lee's manager, Jerry Schilling, who, I was to find out, is perhaps as fascinating as Lewis.

Schilling told me that we were going to go to Jerry Lee's house that night to have dinner. I would be able to walk around the house and look at it to get some ideas for shots. He told me that if Jerry Lee was in a bad mood, we might have to make a quick exit. He said that there was a chance that the interview would not happen if the Killer's temper was flaring. I was also told that if you somehow make him mad, he would reach over to you and flick you in the nose with his finger to see what you would do. Schilling said that he was over there the night before and Lewis had pulled out a large handgun and suggested that the two of them should go down and pay a visit to Sam Phillips, the man who owned and ran Sun Studios, also the man who produced Lewis' most famous sides. Apparently, Jerry Lee felt that the accounting was not up to snuff and wanted to do a drive-by audit.

All of a sudden it was sounding like a bad time – handguns, a true rock legend who apparently does not like to be interviewed – and me.

Schilling told me a bit about himself. He worked for Elvis Presley for eleven years. He lived at Graceland, Elvis' home for as long. Jerry Schilling is the one who took Elvis for his famous meeting with Nixon at the Oval Office. Schilling has stories. I'm sure we'll never know them all. Just the few he laid on me had my head spinning as we drove from Memphis to Nesbit, Mississippi, home of Jerry Lee Lewis.

We drove through the piano-shaped gates of the Lewis Ranch and pulled up near the house. Several cars were parked all over. In the headlights, I could see a lot of dogs get up and walk slowly over to our car. These were some mangy beasts. Some of the Elektra guys were not so hot on the idea of getting out of the car. I was raised with dogs and have this strange idea that all dogs like me. I got right out of the car and started petting all of them. The rest of the guys got out and we and the dogs walked up to the door. Jerry Lee's wife came out and escorted us in.

She said that Jerry Lee wasn't up to coming to the table so we would eat dinner without him. I looked around the living room. It was cool to see Jerry Lee's original Sun gold singles on the wall. They had darkened with age but there they were. I walked into the hallway and saw what was left of his Starck upright piano, the one that his father bought him when he was a child in Ferriday, Louisiana. This is the piano that Jerry Lee played all the way up to his entrance at Sun Studio in 1956. I pulled out the keyboard that was amidst a pile of splintered wood. I opened it up and looked at it. It looked like it had been played for a century by someone who was very angry. All the keys on the right side were worn down past the ivory all the way to the wood screw, and there was dried blood in all the spooned out, demolished keys. I ran my hands over them and tried to imagine him playing on it before there was a genre called Rock & Roll.

Minutes later we sat to dinner and ate some artery clogging, heart stopping food. Jerry Lee's son, Lee, was at the table. He was a total cut-up. As we ate, I looked around the living room. All the furniture was covered in plastic. We were in Mississippi.

We finished and split. I wanted to get back to the hotel and look over my notes a few more times seeing that I was going to be dealing with a guy who could get mad at a moment's notice.

In my room I went over things I had written down back in LA. I already had decided to stay away from his ill-fated trip to England in 1958 where the British press found out that the thirteen year old girl on his arm was not his daughter but his cousin – and *wife*. I heard the Killer gets in a bad mood when asked about that stuff. I was not interested in that. I wanted to know about him and his music, the music that raised him and the influence that religion had on him and his playing. Most of all, I wanted to find out what drove him to go so hard for so long. I wanted to interview the artist that I heard on all those records, that even decades old still inspire awe. His vocal phrasing and piano playing, not to mention the sheer volume of music he has in his head is astounding. He is in full control of his music.

The next morning I met with Matt from the record company and had breakfast before we took off back out to Jerry Lee's to do the interview. I was a little nervous but felt I was ready.

We got into the rental car and a while later we found ourselves in Mississippi and very lost. We were getting close to the time when we were supposed to be there and figured if we were late, Jerry Lee would be waiting for us on his lawn with the gun and the dogs. We pulled into a gas station/department store/convenience mart that advertised a sale on furniture – 'Furnitur Sale'.

I started humming 'Dueling Banjos' from *Deliverance*. We went into the place to get some directions. When we entered, all activity stopped. The locals slowly looked us up and down. We looked so out of place in there it wasn't funny. We asked if anyone knew where the Lewis Ranch was and they all looked at each other and said nothing. Finally, one of them spoke.

'You want to go to Jerry's house?'

'Yes, we were supposed to be meeting him there half an hour ago.'

'You were?'

'Yes. Can you tell us how to get there?'

'Um hum.'

'Ok then, please do.'

'You know that road you were just on?'

'Yeah.'

'You want to go back down it a' ways and you'll see a road? Y'all make a left. Y'all go down that a' ways and you'll see a gate that shaped like a piano? That's where Jerry Lee Lewis lives. Y'all be careful over there.'

We went back to the car and hauled ass over to the house. We were almost an hour late when we got there. Schilling came out and asked us what the hell took us so long. We told him about the 'furnitur sale'.

We went into the house just in time to see Jerry Lee Lewis come out of his room and look at us. I was introduced to him.

I addressed him as 'Mr. Lewis'. He looked right into my eyes when he shook my hand.

Crunch.

Ok, I know who the boss is.

I told him that I was a musician, not a journalist, in the hopes that he might like that better than the idea of talking to a press type. I asked him if he knew what we were doing today and he said that he didn't. He was polite and very humble which threw me off. I explained to him what a video press kit was and that we would be out of here before he knew it. He seemed to like me.

He said, 'Well Hank . . . Do they call you Hank?'

I nodded.

'Well Hank, I'm just gonna let you lead and do my best to keep up with you.'

And with that we hit it.

HR: I want to ask you about your first recordings back in the Sun days and about the time that you went in and recorded 'Crazy Arms' with Jack Clement. It ended up being your first single.

JLL: Me and my dad drove up. I was to meet Mr. Phillips, and Jack Clement was standing there and he said, 'Well, he's not here, he's gone on vacation. Can I help you?' I said, 'Yeah, I want to audition. I play piano and I sing.' He said, 'Well, I never have any time.' And I said, 'Well, you're going to have to take time for this.' I drove a long ways and we didn't have a whole lot of money back then, so kinda in a casual way, he said, 'Well, I got about three or four minutes – tell me what you are going to do.' So I started playing some songs. 'That's pretty good,' he said, 'but can you play a guitar?' [Laughing] 'Yeah, I can play a guitar, but I'm a piano player.' That's how we got into it and to make a long story short, I kinda pushed him into recording 'Crazy Arms'. The only thing he mentioned about 'Crazy Arms' was that the song had been done by four different major artists already. I was, 'Yeah, but let me do it.' I done it my way, and he played it for Mr. Phillips two weeks later, and he released the record.

HR: Back in those days, you didn't have all the luxuries that recording artists do now with digital technology. When you guys were doing it, you had to get it right or you had to do it again. What was that like?

JLL: It made you work a lot harder, and think a lot more about your music. Nowadays, with all the technology they have, it's a completely different ball game – you can hit a flat or sharp note or something and they can bring that note up when they mix it. That don't seem right to me. But, the musicians today, I wouldn't sell them short. There are great musicians, and they've got a lot of talent. But they are spoiled a little bit with the technology. They don't have to, but they go in and record an album for three months.

HR: And you used to do three to five songs a day.

JLL: Yeah. I used to do an album in two and a half hours – three hours at the most. All my albums were like that, except this last one.

HR: I listen a lot to the complete Sun sessions box set of your work, and when there would be three takes of one song, it was interesting to listen to how you would approach it. The first take seemed as if you and the band were just getting used to it and you were trying out different vocals. Then around take three or so, you really stepped into it and it was the master take. There just seemed to be something different that happened to your voice when you're really in the pocket. All of a sudden, it was a Jerry Lee Lewis record.

JLL: I didn't record them to release on record, they've done that years later when I wasn't around. They just released anything they had, remixed it several times, added stuff to it. But what you're talking about is right, at the fourth or fifth lick when we got into it, what I was trying to do was to get the band in tune.

HR: On the new record, you used a more contemporary or modern approach. There are a lot of different people playing on the record.

JLL: Yeah, it was completely different than anything I'd ever done.

HR: It's real powerful and it doesn't sound overdone; it's pure. Two songs I wanted to ask you about are 'Just Down The Road A Piece', and 'House Of Blue Light'. Those are some of the first songs you ever played.

JLL: That's right. I have been asked before to do those songs years ago, but I'd done them back when I was just a kid learning to play the piano. And I used to do 'Down The Road A Piece', and 'House Of Blue Light'. I thought I should just do it the way I used to do it back when I was a kid, but I didn't. I done it the way they wanted to do it. Surprisingly, it come out pretty good, I guess.

HR: It came out real good. Can you tell me anything that you remember from when you used to go to Haney's Big

House to see all those bands, the people you used to see there and who had a really big impact on you?

JLL: I saw B.B. King play there when I was about nine or ten years old – he was like 18 or 19, and he was really laying down some heavy stuff. I used to sneak in and listen to him. I got thrown out a couple of times, but I always made it back in.

HR: And this was where you found the music you wanted to pursue?

JLL: Well, I knew this was in the direction I wanted to go. I loved it. It was boogie-woogie. It wasn't called rock 'n' roll at the time.

HR: It's 1995. Do you have a sense of yourself as to where you stand in contemporary music, the impact you've had on people playing rock 'n' roll today?

JLL: I have heard a lot of the younger musicians – and some are big artists – I heard them with the piano riffs, and the background of the music. Yeah, I can hear a lot of Jerry Lee Lewis stuff there. I think it's complimentary, you know?

HR: So how many shows do you average a year?

JLL: Seventy-five, one hundred shows a year.

HR: That's strong. What is it in you that brings you back to keep playing, to keep giving so much of yourself to all these people all over the world for over forty years now? What brings you back to do this year after year?

JLL: Well, the audience has a lot to do with it, but I don't know, it's just a god-given talent, a raw talent that's still there. I just love it. I can hit the stage, I do my show, never do it exactly the same way. I always change my show up. And you always see a good hour, hour and a half show out of Jerry Lee Lewis. And rock 'n' roll, that old gut-feelin' rock 'n' roll, gettin' on with it, with the program – that's what they want to hear.

HR: It's amazing how long you've done it. You know, rock 'n' roll is a hard living.

JLL: But like you're talkin' about the jazz drummers and musicians that know what's going on. I mean, they can play anything, get into it. They can play some beats and things that are very dangerous. But rock 'n' roll is just a heavy beat like Chuck Berry and Elvis Presley or Jerry Lee Lewis, and people like that. But, yeah, it's hard to do but you've got to do it.

HR: Would you tell a little bit about how your religious beliefs made your music strong?

JLL: Well, I asked the same question to Elvis Presley, who was raised up in the same church I was raised up in, the Pentecostal Assembly of God Church. We learned the same songs in the same way, and we done them with an uptempo beat, and it was a spiritual-type, religious-type music. It was some of the best music in the world. In church, I knew all the music. Then you take it and go away from it to 'Whole Lotta Shakin''. You still got the same beat, the same feel, that religious undertone feelin'.

HR: I'd like to talk a little bit about the early days when Sun was starting up. You and Elvis were contemporaries. What was the feeling back in those days? Was it a feeling of everyone working together?

JLL: We just had a good time. Whenever we got together, we just had a party. We sang our songs and did our thing. We'd do five or six hours at a time, and there was no hostility there as far as jealousy goes or anything like that. That was me and Elvis Presley. We were friends, *good* friends. Music was our life.

HR: You were trying to do stuff with music that really hadn't been done before. Did you run into difficulties trying to explain to people what you meant?

JLL: Yeah, very much so. They looked at me like I'm crazy, I couldn't get through to them.

HR: Taking gospel tunes and cutting them to boogie time, you must have people thinking you're . . .

JLL: Spiritual . . .

HR: Crazy . . .

JLL: Right! I call that spiritual music. You call it boogie. I guess I put a boogie touch to it.

HR: You've got a lot of gold and platinum records here. You've had so many gold singles, and I don't think a lot of people really know that you had singles on the R&B, country and pop charts all at once. That's the most ultimate crossover thing anyone's ever done.

JLL: We had twelve singles in the Billboard Top 100 at one time. These were the first gold records I ever received: 'Whole Lotta Shakin' ', 'Great Balls of Fire', 'Breathless', 'High School Confidential'.

We go over to the Starck piano that sits against the wall in pieces.

HR: Can we talk about this piano?

JLL: People moved this old piano, and they didn't know it was so old. I've got to get it put back together. This is my original. This is the piano my mama and daddy bought for me when I was eight years old, and nobody played this piano but me. I put the holes in the ivory, cause that's real ivory on those keys.

HR: The blood and all is from you just pounding it?

JLL: That's right, they got it from me playing.

HR: You'd take it to shows?

JLL: Well, we'd take it to church revivals and those things, and car shows, different things.

HR: Are you going to have it restored?

JLL: Yeah, they're gonna bring it back to its originality. I'm not going to change it in any way except put it back together. It was a player piano but it was redone for a regular piano by some people in Monroe, Louisiana, and my folks went over and bought it for me. Great memories there – memories you live on.

HR: Cool! Can we take a walk down the hall? There are a couple of things I want to ask you about. [*We look at some photographs.*] So this is your father's father? Is this the man who had knocked the horse down with his fist?

JLL: No, no, no, that would be my great-great-great-grandfather, ha-ha-ha.

HR: So this is your father's father?

JLL: Right. He was a little bitty short fellow and my dad was like six-foot-five, a big man. My father could pick up my grandfather. And this is my mother and me and my brother, who got killed when he was nine years old.

We look at a picture of a drugstore.

HR: Tell me about that.

JLL: Well, when we got out of school, anywhere from the first grade on up to the tenth grade, we would always stop by there, have a milkshake or a Salty Dog. That wasn't an alcoholic drink, a Salty Dog. It was one of the greatest drinks in the world.

This picture in the pool hall goes back to 1949. You can see me leaning up against the slot machine with the sailor cap on. Yeah, I shot a many game of pool.

HR: That's you and Buddy Holly?

JLL: Uh-huh. Me and Buddy, sitting at the piano. We were in Australia when that picture was taken. He was very much one of my best friends, Buddy Holly.

HR: What do you remember of him?

JLL: He was one of the nicest people I ever met. He was one of a kind. He was a clean-cut, all-American boy. He didn't curse, he didn't smoke, he didn't drink. I was beginning to wonder if he ever went out with girls, but I think he did.

HR: Here's a picture with you and Kris Kristofferson. I know you've done some of his songs. You must have a great respect for him.

JLL: I sure do. He's one of my best friends. He is good people.

HR: Do people send you paintings of you and stuff like that?

We look at a picture where Jerry Lee is sitting at the piano at a gig, looking absolutely crazed.

JLL: Yeah, they do, paintings and stuff. It looks like somebody took a lot of pills! [*Laughter all around.*]

HR: A lot of live shots. It looks like you honestly still enjoy playing.

JLL: Yeah, I do, I do. I love playing. That's my life.

HR: That's why you keep changing the sets and everything, just to keep it interesting and spontaneous?

JLL: It's got to be different. I just like to go up and try out different songs.

HR: And at this point, you must know so many.

JLL: Yeah, it's like I told Kenny Loveless, he's been working with me for nearly 30 years now. I said, 'Kenny, every night I can play a song that you have never heard me do before.' I can still do that.

HR: This is some spread here, Jerry. Let me tell you, it's beautiful.

JLL: Yeah, this is a great place. It needs a lot of work done now, but when I first bought it twenty-three years ago, it was so pretty.

HR: It must be nice to be able to come off the road and come back here.

JLL: It's peaceful down here.

HR: So it's been twelve years since you recorded an album. What was it like to go back in, not having been in that way of thinking for a while?

JLL: Well, I was looking forward to it – I really wanted to record. I thought it was ridiculous to wait that long. It was great to get back in the studio, I tell you that.

HR: Where was it recorded?

JLL: In Memphis, at the studio. I can't think of the name.

HR: Didn't you record some of the stuff here?

JLL: No, we didn't record anything here at the house! We done a lot of studying here, going through rehearsals, but we didn't record anything. I don't *think* they recorded anything. I tell you, I wouldn't bet against it. Nowadays, it's hard to tell when they are recording and when they are not.

HR: You want to talk about any of the players on the record? Some of these people are really well-known. Did you pick any players? Did you request some old friends?

JLL: We just kind of picked them together, me and Andy Paley. Kenny Loveless played on it, and James Burton, who worked with Elvis.

HR: You want to talk a little bit about the song, 'Crown Victoria', since it's a song you co-wrote on the record?

JLL: Yeah. Andy (Andy Paley, *Young Blood*'s producer) and me was sitting down, talking about what would be a special kind of automobile you always wanted but you could never have. I said, 'Well, they didn't make it but it would have been a 1951 Crown Victoria.' They made the Crown Victoria in 1955. If they would have made it in 1951, they would have had a heck of an automobile! So we wrote the song around that.

HR: And 'Goose Bumps' is the first single. Does that feel good to you to have that as the lead single?

JLL: I have to listen to it a couple more times. Every time I listen to it, I say, 'I don't know' and then I listen to it again and think 'Yeah, that's it!'

Jerry Lee's eight year old son Lee comes into the room.

JLL: There's a young man looking for trouble! How you doing, baby? Good day in school?

Lee: I got all As on my . . .

JLL: Oh, well, that's great, baby!

HR: So who's this?

Lee: Lee Lewis.

HR: So what's it like having your dad be Mr. Jerry Lee Lewis?

Lee: Oh, great.

HR: Do you ever listen to any of your dad's records?

Lee: Yeah.

HR: So what do you think of your dad's new album?

Lee: I haven't really heard it yet, so I don't know.

JLL: I haven't had him listen to the new album yet. I'm scared he might give me a frank answer.

HR: What do you want to get out of this record? Do you want to see young people check this record out and discover your music?

JLL: I believe the younger generation will get into this record. I think they've been waiting. They have been buying all this old song stuff that they've been re-releasing. They have been buying a gallon, a bucketful of them things. So they are going to buy this album, I believe.

HR: I think it's a real important record because I think you're someone whom people should listen to.

JLL: Well, thank you.

The high point was toward the end when he sat down at the piano in his living room and was convinced by Jerry Schilling to play a little for the camera. The Killer said that the piano was out of tune and he wouldn't be able to make

'Jerry Lee Lewis music' with it. He was told that the sound
was not going to be used, other music was going to be laid
over it. This seemed to be ok with him. I put my elbow
down on the top of the piano like Steve Allen used to do
on his television show. Jerry Lee flipped up the cover of
the keyboard and his entire body language changed right
in front of me. It was like an electro-chemical reaction. He
seemed to increase in size. He threw his head back and his
hands slammed down on the keys and he started man-
handling them like he was trying to see if they could be
broken. It was intense as hell to be a foot away from this
energy surge. It's something that I'll never forget. All at
once he stopped playing and got up from the piano with
disdain like it was a vanquished foe. We all instinctively
jumped back a little.

We took some pictures together and he told me that I
was welcome to come by and visit any time. I asked him
if he felt ok about the whole thing and he said he was
impressed with my questions and research.

'You sure did your homework, killer.'

We said goodbye and left. Jerry Schilling asked us if we
wanted to visit Graceland. The Elektra guys wanted to go
so we went. We pulled into the parking lot of the offices
located near Graceland and walked in. When the people
in there saw Schilling, they had a panic attack. They all
ran up to him and hugged him like he was some son
returning from war. I guess he's a big deal there. He asked
if he could take his friends from New York on a little tour
through the house. One of the staff, a young woman who
seemed to be really happy – happy like she was in a cult
kind of happy – drove us over to Graceland in her car. The
front seat was littered with tapes – ALL ELVIS. One of the

Elektra guys looked at us and then looked at her and asked, 'So what kind of music do you listen to?' She said that she listened to all kinds. 'All kinds of Elvis,' I thought to myself. She was intense.

When we pulled up to the front gate, Presley's version of 'What'd I Say?' blaring, I asked, 'Is this the gate that Jerry Lee Lewis pulled up at all fucked up, waving a handgun telling the guard, "Wake fat boy up, tell him the Killer is here!"?' She looked at me blankly with a pasted on smile.

When we got to the house, I saw the scene I had always pictured when I thought of visiting Graceland. The front and side of the house were littered with the most regressive people I had ever seen. Women in bright stretch pants, traumatized men and children wandering around suffering the effects of what looked like too many years of drinking water that ran past a Dow Chemical plant. I said, 'Look at these people, they're all insane! Ohmigod look at those clothes!' Our cheery office tour guide looked at them and reeled off statistics of how many people come to Graceland daily, weekly and yearly. She didn't seem to notice that they were all mutants.

We went in and Jerry started showing us around. A few minutes in he seemed to be getting a little shook up. I guessed that the place holds a lot of memories for him. It must be weird to see the place you lived in for eleven years turned into a museum.

It was wild to look at the pictures of Elvis everywhere and see Jerry standing there with him. He took us to his old room but the door was locked. By the time we had gone through the house he excused himself. We found out later that it was the third time he had been back there since Presley had died. The first time was to take Priscilla there after Elvis Presley's death and a few months before our visit when a Presley died. I thought that it was great that he took us there considering what it was doing to him emotionally.

We went into a small house on the property that Elvis and the boys used for target practice. In there is an office where Elvis was interviewed once and the place is still intact and there is a television playing the interview. We stood and watched the television for a while. The most interesting part about it was the office girl. She was standing next to me mouthing every word that came out of Elvis' mouth and laughing at his aw shucks humor as she mouthed the little aside to herself. I wondered what she would be like in bed. No, let's not go there.

We saw some other stuff – the room with the gold and platinum records all the way to the ceiling. I was getting bored. I never cared for Elvis after he made the Sun recordings. The most interesting part of the whole tour to me was Jerry Schilling.

We got back in the car and heard the rest of 'What'd I Say?' as we went back to the offices. We said goodbye and Jerry took us to the airport. A few hours later I was sitting on the edge of a hotel room bed in Manhattan wondering if all of that had really happened to me in one day.

Post Script: Months later I got a call from Jerry Schilling asking about MTV. Apparently 'the Big M' was not interested in having Jerry Lee Lewis on their *120 Minutes* show. I told him to tell them that I would interview Jerry Lee and see if they went for that.

They did and on May 17, 1995, I met up with Mr. Lewis and Mr. Schilling and we went into the MTV building. On the way in Jerry Lee said to me, 'Hank, this is an honor. MTV is what all the kids are watching.' I could not explain to him that it was an honor for MTV to have someone like him there. He didn't seem to understand his weight in this place. He was as nervous as the staff. It was strange to see him be so quiet.

We did the interview one question at a time. I would tell him what I was going to ask him and then we would shoot it. It took a while but we got through it ok. Never once did he seem relaxed there. I think he really felt out of place.

I have read a lot about Jerry Lee. A lot of the press types talk about his big ego. I think that he has a lot of pride about what he does, and what he has made, and what he has survived. To stand in his shoes as long as he has you have to be one tough bastard. If you read about the ups and downs the man has experienced in his life, it's pretty hard to believe that he went through it all. The people who write poorly about him have no clue what that kind of intensity is like. I agree that he is full of himself, like a lot of great performers. I think a lot of it is a raging self-belief – what you need to keep going out there night after night, through good times and bad, for decades.

All you have to do is listen to Jerry Lee's Sun sessions or the *Live at the Hamburg Star Club* CD and it makes you realize the demonic energy of this guy. He was much more of a threat to parents than any of these contemporary posers. When Jerry Lee was starting out, people would tell him that he was making the Devil's Music. Jerry Lee, being raised religiously, really believed it. He was putting his soul on the line. He really thought he was going to go to Hell for the music he was making. He made it anyway.

He had it all and lost it all and still kept on playing. The IRS has emptied his house twice. He is on the tightest leash they give. He has to do a certain amount of shows a year to keep the cash flow happening or they threaten to take it all away for good. Sixty years old and still in trouble.

The guy is a maniac but that's what rock and roll was supposed to be about, right? Crazy folks and the music that made them that way. He's the real thing and at this point we can all kiss his ass if we don't like it. Rock and Roll will never die.

Originally appeared in RAYGUN

HARD COFFEE BLUES

11.19.95 Afternoon LA CA: It is Sunday and it's kind of a day off for me The week was pretty stressed and I'm glad I made it through. I had four shows in four days which normally isn't a big deal to me. The first two of the four were a bit trying. The first was last Wednesday when the band played under the name 'The Theo Van Rock Experience' at CBGB's to kick some new songs and play live before we played in Australia. It was the first time in my life I had not been totally prepared to play with the band. Not all the lyrics were set and I had to bring some notes onstage with me. I have never done this before in my life. For a good part of the set, I was improvising and I think I pulled it off rather well but setting up for it had me stressing pretty bad. The next hurdle was the next night when I was to do a talking show at the Beacon Theater uptown. The gig had over two thousand tickets sold and the movie agent was coming out from LA as well as management and all kinds of press people and all the people who they invited. I knew I was going to treat it like any other show and give them the best I had. I think that any performer who gives it up for some towns more than others should just quit. And though I never usually feel any nerves at all about going onstage, this was day two of stage nerves – a new thing for me.

The show was a blast, the audience was great and I think I did well. It was a relief to have those shows done. Next stop was two dates in Wisconsin, a state I really like playing in. Those were good shows although I thought I was somewhat distracted at the Milwaukee show on account of sound problems and some drunks. Otherwise it was cool.

So now I'm here for about a day and a half. Basically a stopover on my way to Australia for four shows in five days.

It's nice to be here I guess. I like having access to my records. I miss playing them. Problem is that when I am here I can rarely decide what to play. It's always a race against the clock to squeeze in as much down time as possible before the next trip starts. I have disconnected the phone and I feel very good about that.

Several weeks ago I got a call from a television station in Melbourne, Australia. They told me about a young guy, seventeen years old, named Marius Bannister. Marius has leukemia and is fighting for his life in a local hospital. They asked him what he wanted and he said that he wanted to meet me. They found out that I was going to be in Melbourne and asked if I would go and hang out with Marius for a while on the day off after the show. Of course I said I would. I have no idea what I'll say to the guy but I can't say no to that. I wonder what that must be like. Seventeen years is no age to be messed up in a hospital bed.

11.22.95 8:49 p.m. Sydney Australia I flew in from LA several hours ago. I timed the flight with my stopwatch, 14:05:36. I must have slept for most of it. I did read a good portion of Truman Capote's *Music for Chameleons* – an excellent read.

On my flight were Melvin, Sim, and Tim, our monitor man. Chris, Rick, our road manager, and Ken, our drum technician, came in on an earlier flight. We are staying at the Gazebo Hotel in King's Cross. We went to a place to eat down the street from here called Hard Coffee. What a great name for a place, Hard Coffee. The coffee and the food were good.

I spent most of the day walking around looking in book and record stores. My main purpose was to stay awake. Now it's night time and my hotel window looks out over a non-descript piece of street. It's raining fairly hard and I am in my room sagging. I have the television on and the Beatles special is on. It's a drag to listen to chirpy Paul McCartney prattle away about the band and how it was. The live parts of the documentary were great. What an undeniably incredible band they were, you can't mess with it. I can't listen to the Beatles anymore. It is hard for me to listen to John Lennon's voice – all I can think about is how he died for nothing. I can't listen to Nirvana – it makes me too mad and empty. I am sick of dead rockstars. Shannon Hoon's death filled me with anger and empty, dark loneliness.

The way Chapman took out Lennon makes me too mad to be able to stand the music for too long. Chapman is such a wormy little bastard. It's too bad that he was allowed to live. It's not as if he really had any passion about what he did either. I remember at some point after Lennon was dead, Chapman was interviewed and he just mumbled some lightweight bullshit about *The Catcher in the Rye*. He took out one of the good ones. All the other Beatle solo records make me sick. David Geffen told me he was with Lennon the night he was killed. That must have rocked his world pretty hard. How could you kill John Lennon?

It's good to be out of the states for a while. We have four shows coming up in a couple of days. I have been doing speaking dates all over the place lately and it's good to get a break from them as well. Twenty-eight shows since September. They are hard to do and they leave me drained, exhausted and wired. The response has been good. It's great when I get a letter from someone saying that they just saw me and it inspired them to work harder at what they do. It's good to get someone out of the dumps, even if it's only for a little while.

11.23.95 Sydney Australia We had band practice today in the usual place. We always end up there. The Cruel Sea was practicing next door. It was good to talk to their singer, Tex Perkins. I haven't seen him in a while. Practice was good. I like the new songs – they get better the more we play them.

I went to the gym and got a good workout. The walk through the King's Cross neighborhood was wild as always. I watched a young girl take an old man to a room. The Cross is always full of freaks. The Samoan man with the scarred eyebrows and flattened nose. The men dressed as women smiled at me when I stared at their stomachs hanging out of their shirts.

Now I'm in the room. The rest of the band is out eating somewhere. I didn't go because it would have messed with the workout. I am glad to be on my own. It's a relief. Soon I'll go out for a walk to try to stay awake.

11.24.95 Sydney Australia Played tonight at the University of Wollongong. It was hard going. I don't think I have ever heard so much feedback in one gig in my life. It was a tour's worth of feedback up there. Everywhere I went with the mic, I was howling away. The crowd was great and we had The Mark of Cain as openers and they tore it up as usual. Babes in Toyland played as well and they were good.

I liked the drive home because all the guys were telling stories about past tours. They were talking about the scariest drives and someone mentioned a ride in South America last year and another talked about the hell drives in Moscow. It was cool to hear these stories because it made me realize that we have made a small history for ourselves. We have our own legend that belongs only to us. Experiences that we have shared and can recall and laugh about that no one can really get to past a certain level. This is us. This is not something that we are doing until we chicken out and go to college. This is our lives and this is what we do. The wet highway hisses underneath us and the laughter bounces off the roof as we speed back to Sydney. This is a good life. As bad as it gets, we have beaten the everyday grind and are living it our way.

My body aches – first gig afterburn. Head feels like it's going to explode. Neck stiff. Ribs hurt from me punching and clawing myself. Entering Sydney city limits at night always reminds me of driving into London after a show. Always tired and always a ways off from sleep. Your head bounces off your chest and you have a slight panic attack because you wake up thinking that you are the one driving. I am not lonely even though I have not touched a woman in a long time. I feel fine inside myself. I don't know why I feel so completely fine right now. Most likely it is the pain that is shooting through my body as I sit and write this. It's the pain that lets me know that I played hard and gave them all I had. It is an honor to be on this warrior path. Even if no one sees it this way but me.

11.25.95 Brisbane Australia I am in one of my favorite hotels in one of the most beautiful places I have ever seen. Brisbane, Australia is stunning to the eye. It is a beautiful night. Cool and dry. The night is clear to perfection. The view off the balcony is the harbor and the skyline. Boats are tied. The stars are clearly defined. It is quiet and amazing.

I wish I didn't have to get up in the morning early and hit the road to Melbourne. It would be great to stay up all night. If I ever took time off, it would be here.

We played the Livid Festival tonight. It was a pretty good time but I don't think that we played all that well. It was a good show not a great one. It was hell for us because there was no soundcheck and the monitors were feeding back like crazy. Not as bad as last night which might set the record for feedback hell we have experienced.

Tonight's show was typical for festivals in that you just have to go for it and play your ass off and not care about how it sounds onstage since there is not enough time to get it together. The drag was the people bothering me all day. I don't mind people but when they're drunk and in my face when I'm trying to get ready to play or when I'm trying to catch my breath after the show and they start in with the bullshit, it is no fun. It's hard to be nice to people when they are in your face not respecting your space. They make me want to smack one of them so the rest can see that they shouldn't fuck with me. I don't have any sympathy for drunks in my face. Fuck 'em. The audience however, was fantastic. They went as hard as we did.

It's an honor to play in Australia, the audiences are great.

Otherwise, it's good to be playing. It will be good to have Theo back with us. His father died so he has been in Holland for the last few days sorting it out. He gets here in the morning.

Body doesn't hurt as much as yesterday. I guess it's getting used to the pounding. Another one awaits.

11.26.95 Melbourne Australia Another amazing night. This time the air is slightly more moist and the smell of the ocean is more present. The show went off well. Very enthusiastic people there. After the show I went out the back with the rest of the guys to leave and there were people waiting for us by the van as usual. Things have changed with the post-show ritual in the last couple of years. Now there's security guys everywhere and I have to tell them that it's ok for people to come up and get things signed or take a photo. The whole thing is a lot more strange than it used to be. Some of the kids who were waiting for us ran after the van all the way to the hotel.

About half an hour later, me and the rest of the guys walked down Fitzroy Street in search of food. They went to a pizza place and I went further up the block to an all night market I have been to before. I went in and one guy ran in after me yelling my name. He was pretty drunk. The store owner asked him to leave. I tried to tell the kid that I would talk to him as soon as I got out of the store, but by that time the owner and the kid had gotten into a tussle and were knocking stuff off the shelves. Meanwhile, some other people had come in and were around me. It all turned into a bad situation in no time. I got out of there after exchanging apologies with the store owner. I went outside to talk to these youths. A few of them were drunk as hell and not making much sense. I signed a few of their shirts and split. I don't see why you would want to waste your time being so fucked up. How incredibly boring and depressing.

The other night I had come off stage in Brisbane and I was sitting in a chair in front of the trailer that was our dressing room. I was cooling off and settling down. A few minutes into this, it occurred to me that people were really great to not bother me right after a show. I thought, 'How considerate of them to let a guy catch his breath and not get in his face minutes after he has walked off a stage.' It was then I noticed that there were four security guards stationed around me and there were people in front of them waving pieces of paper for me to sign. All of a sudden it turned into a bad scene. I don't want to be protected by security – that makes me feel weak. But at the same time, I don't want to get bugged so soon after playing. It angers me that people are rarely considerate of the backstage. I figure that if you're back there, you shouldn't bug a performer and should not ask for autographs. The backstage is the only place a guy in a band can be left alone. When you take that away, then you should expect the worst from anyone in that position.

I'm here in the room wishing I could stay up all night. I am tired and sore and my throat is pretty scorched.

11.27.95 Melbourne Australia Today I visited Marius Bannister. A guy from the television station came and picked me and Rick up at the hotel and took us to the hospital where he has been for several months.

When I got to his room, a nurse was there and she made me wash my hands so I would not infect him with my handshake.

She told me a few things about Marius' appearance so I wouldn't be alarmed when I saw him. I was told that due to the chemotherapy, his lips were chapped and the inside of his mouth was ulcerated and he would bleed slightly when he spoke. She went on to tell me that no one had told him that I was in town and was going to visit him. She knocked on his door and asked him if it was alright to bring in a visitor. I heard someone say yes and I went in.

When I walked in, he was pretty surprised. He sat up, looked at me and said, 'Fuck!' and we shook hands. The nurse and the television guy left us alone and I sat on the edge of his bed and we started talking. I didn't know what to say to a young man who is fighting for his life. What can you and all your years and wisdom say to a seventeen year old boy who has tubes coming out of his chest, no hair left from the chemotherapy, ulcerating gums and nothing but his guts to live on? What the hell do you say?

He was telling me how it was for him and every time he enunciated a word I could see blood on his teeth. He told me that sometimes it was hard to keep the strength up to fight it off and that on some days he gets scared. He said that when his parents and friends came to visit him, he keeps up a good front and tries to smile because they mean well. He said at night he gets scared to sleep because he's afraid to die in his sleep. He said that if he was going to die, he wanted to be awake. That was one of the most intense things I have ever heard someone say. Seventeen years old and he is in a place where it occurs to him to say something like that. I realized at that moment that he was stronger than I'll ever be. I knew who was in charge of the conversation. I immediately felt like a child sitting with a wise elder.

He started shaking and almost broke down and I changed the subject and we started talking about what he was going to do when he got the hell out of there. I told him I thought that he was looking really good and knew that he was going to beat the hell out of this thing and I honestly did believe that. He already had two of his friends in his ward die. It must be hard to take.

We talked for a while about things in general. I saw that he had a poster of the Beastie Boys on the wall so I told him what cool people they were and how we had toured with them.

After a while we ran out of things to say and he asked me what I was going to do that day and I told him I was going to hang out with an old friend of mine but that I would write him when I got back to America.

I told him that he was on the guest list for the next show and that I'd see him next time. We exchanged addresses and the nurse took a photo of the two of us.

On my way out the door, he told me that he had wanted to meet me for years and I was exactly as he thought I would be and I didn't let him down. I know that he has no idea what a flawed and wretched person I can be.

I met his father and his grandmother outside the room. They thanked me for coming and then Rick and I left. It was a strange way to start the day. It took me a while to get the smell of the hospital out of my nose. I hate those places.

When I got back to the room, I called Mick Geyer. He's a long standing friend of mine. Whenever I am in

Melbourne, we hang out as much as possible and fill each other in on records and books that we have found since last seeing each other. He is an encyclopedia on good music, film and literature. I always come away from his place with a stack of new things to watch, listen to and read. He is one who turned me onto Slim Gaillard, James Ellroy, Don Pullen, David Murray, Louis Jordan, Julius Hemphill, Nelson Algren, the list goes on.

He walked over to where I was and we set off in search of food and coffee. We spent the day talking about everything and, as always, it was a fascinating time. I always take notes. We listened to the new Bad Seeds stuff that he had gotten from Nick – mixes of *The Murder Ballads* album. We went to a few bookstores and showed books to each other. I turned him onto Max Frisch. He picked up *Homo Faber* and *I'm Not Stiller*.

I hung out with Mick until almost midnight and then walked back here to the room. I wanted to stay longer but I have to travel in the morning.

Hanging with Mick makes me think of life and death. How you get to tell your story and then die. With Mick, it all flows and it's all real. Books, CDs and records line his shelves. More books are piled on almost every flat surface. The names and topics weave together in spontaneous flow – Coltrane, Francis Bacon, Democracy, James Agee, Ennio Morricone, Blake, John Cale, Diamanda Galas, Gorecki, Mingus, Euripides, Shakespeare, Miyamoto Musashi, Slavery, Sonny Rollins, Mikal Gilmore, Gil Evans, Nico, Roky Erickson – the language goes on. Travel, America, England, Greece. The hours pass – it is good.

If I lose the light of the sun, I will write by candlelight, moonlight, no light. If I lose paper and ink, I will write in blood on forgotten walls. I will write always. I will capture nights all over the world and bring them to you. Like this Melbourne night. A sliver of moon hangs against blue-black clear star packed sky. The smell of nearby water. Lit coastline. Traffic goes by. A large fruit bat flies crookedly overhead. Whistling and hooting drunks coming back from the dead end bars on Fitzroy pass by several yards away.

Night is the harvester of memories. Night is the gatherer of thoughts that hide in sunlight. Night brings out the inhabitants from the deep cracks that shun the idiotic noise of the masses. Night empowers and makes one bold. True love and the telling of secrets only happens at night. Sunlight is a passionless interrogator. Candlelight brings out the beauty of the human form.

11.29.95 Sydney Australia Tonight was the last show and I thought we played well. I had a great time and the audience was great as well. Sim lost some major portions of skin from his hand and had to tough it out for the gig. He pulled it off but he seemed to be in a lot of pain afterwards. Sim plays with pain often and doesn't complain.

In the morning, I leave for the States. It's past two in the morning and I am fried. I walked around King's Cross tonight to get some food. What a scene. Even on a Tuesday night it's live.

I was thinking about Washington DC as I walked around. The smell in the air reminded me of springtime there. I can always think fondly of my hometown when I am far from there but I noticed when I was actually there a few weeks ago I felt strange and sad in a way. Only from a distance can I think of the place with any clarity. I wonder why the hell that is.

Excerpt from notebook: I am writing this down to not forget the events. On October 26, I went to Washington DC. I had a show the next night and there was no band practice on the day before so I figured I would go early and check out the old hometown not having been there since August 21, 1994. I got there in the evening and checked into the hotel which is located at Calvert and Wisconsin.

I went out for a walk around ten p.m. It was strange as always to walk down Wisconsin Ave. The pet shop I once worked at has been vacated by the Italian restaurant that was there. They moved down the street to a bigger place. I stood in front of the window and stared in for quite a while. I kept walking, all the while noticing that even more things had changed since the last time I had been there. I walked past all my old places of employment and walked to Tower Records in Foggy Bottom. The streets had lost all their familiarity and I was starting to feel displaced and slightly depressed. On the way there, I saw a young man playing go-go beats on a setup of plastic barrels on M Street. I listened to him for some time and moved on. He was great.

I spent a long time in the record store which is an easy thing for me to do. Such a loner I am, who would have me?! I ate at the place inside the building that contains the record store and started back to the hotel. I walked up and down some old streets. As always, the streets at night were beautiful. I walked up 31st Street a ways and looked at the houses I used to deliver papers to over twenty years ago. The color of the leaves and the street lamp glow were amazing. There was no one on the street but me and it was like I was on a movie set. The houses looked like a dream shrouded in the soft light and leaves.

I walked back to the hotel and went to my room. Next day I was up as early as I could. I walked back down Wisconsin to R Street, past one of the apartments I grew up in and down 30th Street. I went through the alley behind R Street and through another to 31st Street. I walked back to the hotel via the Boy's Club. I ate in a place that used to be the deli I hung out in when I was a teen. I worked out in the gym down the street and a few hours later, I was on a stage doing a talking show at the Lisner Auditorium. I went back to the hotel afterwards and left the next morning for Cincinnati. It was a relief to be moving again.

Besides the show, it was a complete letdown to go there. It was depressing as hell. I walked by the houses of people that I had known and I couldn't remember which house they were in. I felt like I had gone back in time and was not welcome. There was absolutely no romance with the place that I can so easily summon up when I am in a place like Australia. Only when I am far away does it seem like a nice place to be. I guess it will just be a place in my head. If I was there now, I know I would be looking to get out of there.

When I was there, all I could think about were my parents and how life used to be for me. I despise my early years so much. The streets brought it all back. Seeing the places I used to wait for my father to pick me up for the court-sanctioned weekend visit. The strangeness of *that* and how fake it all seemed. Like they were doing me a favor or just doing the job now that they had a child.

I do not hate my parents. I do not think they are bad people. I believe that they did the best they could and worked hard to raise me right. But I cannot help the feeling of suffocation when I think of the way we raised each other. I was not a good son. I never knew what the 'son' role was about because I guess I could never figure out what theirs was supposed to be. It would be great to go to them, whip out a checkbook and say, 'Ok, the childhood. Food, clothes, books, quality time, toilet training, etc. How much? Ok, there you go. Good doing business with you.' I think that would be such a righteous way to deal with all of that. It does boil down to pay for time and materials in my mind. Perhaps I am not much of a son.

The strange thing is that I have been back there before and the feeling was not the same. Perhaps it is because I have always hung out with Ian when I have visited there and it's a different thing when he's around. It's more fun and I am less self-involved.

Spending time with Ian MacKaye is a thing I place on a top priority level. It's such an amazing piece of luck to have grown up with such an amazing person. It will always be something that I will be shamelessly proud of.

Another thing I learned from this recent visit is that I have truly grown out of the place. The sadness I felt when I was last there could very well be my coming to terms with the fact that I have indeed gone on with my life and the place is part of my past. I have a strange relationship with my past. I basically got up and left town to go join this crazy rock band and never came back. When I see Ian, I always feel like I'm still checking it out and might be coming 'home' soon. In some ways, I probably did not confront myself in that I indeed did get up and go and never came back. Perhaps DC represents a less complicated time of my life. The last fifteen years have been intense to say the least.

Unless Ian is in town, I don't think I'll be going back there unless it's to perform. There's nothing there but memories – bad ones at that.

I have a long way to go before I get to LA. A few days from now I'm back on the spoken trail working my way back to NYC right into band practice. I have to go to sleep. It was a good trip.

Too bad we have to leave, I think we were just getting warmed up.

Several hours later: I'm sitting in a coffee place at the airport, listening to three men talk about their time in Vietnam. Waiting for the flight. Thinking about my hometown. No thoughts about women like I used to. I don't get lonely like I used to. It's like a huge leech has been taken off me. I can just be on my own and be fine with it. I like this very much.

Taste of coffee in my mouth. Feet full of blisters from the shows. The vets talk about where they're going. They will be on my flight. Their talk is mundane – fishing, clothes, alcohol percentages in Australian beers.

Now almost ten hours into the flight. Time has passed fairly quickly even though I have not slept yet. The shows were good. It was strange to be there for only four shows and then pack it all up and go home. So many rituals that you fall into when you tour with the same people year after year. The long running in-jokes and the gig rituals. Like when Theo comes backstage and tells us he's going to the soundboard and he tells us to 'rock out'. When Tim gives me a fresh mic every few songs and we say 'Thank you, sir' to each other every time. And of course, the nonstop awesomeness of our road manager Rick Smith, who just defies categorization and manages to say things every year that will make you blush. A few days in, it's like we never left the road. On this one, it was weird to be in that sphere for a minute and then to go back home, jilted out of the little world that we make for ourselves every time we go out there.

Seven hours or so later: I'm back in my room in LA. The beast smiled at me as I drove through its guts to my doorstep. I always feel hunted in this town. The beast knows when I land and how long I plan to stay. It decides if it will allow me to live. Another journey is over. All I think about is getting back to the airport and getting out of here.

4.29.96 NYC NY After meeting Marius, I finished the speaking dates I had scheduled. On many nights, I told people about him. How brave he was and how much I learned from his strength and courage.

A few weeks ago, mail that I received in LA was forwarded out to me. In it was a letter from Marius Bannister's mother. She thanked me for visiting her son and said that I gave him a lot to think about. He died on January 22, 1996.

THE KING'S CALL 1996

12.22.95 LA CA A few months ago, I was asked to take part in the King's Call concert in Dublin, Ireland. The concert, set for January 6, 1996, marks the ten year anniversary of Thin Lizzy's bass player and main song-writer, Phil Lynott's death. Some members of Thin Lizzy are going to play a set and they have asked some people from other bands to sit in. That's where I come in.

I have been asked to sing a song with the band. From what I understand, Def Leppard's Joe Elliott and members of the band Therapy? will be there as well. I don't know which members of the Lizzy will be there. Towards the end of the band's career, they had a few guitarists come and go. The only constant guitar player was the great Scott Gorham, who came a few albums into the band's existence and stayed all the way to the end.

I have been a fan of Thin Lizzy ever since I heard their song 'The Boys Are Back in Town' many years ago. When I go out on tour, I always have at least three hours of Lizzy on tape with me. The band could be the most played rock band on my stereo.

Phil's voice and what he says in the lyrics always inspires me. When I am lonely, nothing gets it like Thin Lizzy. So many nights I have listened to the band as the miles died under the wheels on an overnight drive. It is uncanny how many good songs this band has. Their two guitar attack is a classic sound that has been copied all over the world.

I went to Ireland for the first time in 1992, when we were opening for the Red Hot Chili Peppers. Apparently my love for Thin Lizzy had already made itself known there. I was met at the venue by Smiley Bolger, a friend of Lizzy's who was very cool and told me some Phil stories.

Our road manager Rick Smith, used to hang out with Phil in London at the Marquee, one of Phil's preferred watering holes. He saw the band a lot of times. I had a chance in the seventies when they opened for Queen. I couldn't make the show and have been kicking myself ever since. I remember on my second visit to Dublin in 1993 to do a spoken performance, Rick pointed out a hall in which he had seen Lizzy play. The cab driver turned around and told us about how he used to sometimes pick up Phil and take him home. 'He was a very kind man, but always seemed sad.' I live for these stories. On some of the European tours we have done, we have had a guy named Steve out with us. He was Phil's bass tech on one of the last Lizzy tours. He gave me one of Phil's mirrored pick guards.

I got up early this morning and pulled out all the articles I have on Thin Lizzy and re-read them all to reacquaint myself with some of the facts. I am playing all the band's records today in chronological order as well.

Phil died of blood poisoning due to his hardcore drug and alcohol intake over a several year period. His body just gave out on him. He spent the last week and a half of his life in a hospital bed.

I leave in a few days for Dublin. I have been thinking about this a lot. I guess I will get to meet some of the band members and perhaps Phil's mother, Philomena.

1.1.96 Los Angeles International Airport 11:23 a.m. I slept a few hours and feel alright. I'm starting my journey to Dublin, Ireland. I'll get there tomorrow morning Dublin time. Another long flight. This will be a cool trip. I am looking forward to meeting the guys in Thin Lizzy and seeing Rick Smith, one of the world's greatest people and the best road manager there is. I don't see how he keeps so much together while moving from city to city. I wouldn't touch that job.

People are coming up to me telling me that I was good in *Heat*. I keep forgetting I was in that movie. I don't really think about the fact that people go to see movies that I am in. I just do the work and keep moving. I think I was in that movie for about eighty seconds total. They could have gotten anyone to do that part. There was nothing to it besides getting knocked around. It was cool though and it was a blast to work with Al Pacino. LAX is full of people. Flights leaving to Tokyo and Osaka on either side of me. A flight to Hong Kong a few gates up.

Every time I leave LA, I get in a good mood. I can't help it. The cab driver told me that he never wants to see another city as long as he lives. He wants to stay here for the rest of his life. I can see him getting old in this city. Los Angeles makes old people look corny. It strips the elderly of their dignity. They don't look like people who went through World War II. They look like they were hatched out of strip mall nightmares.

Last night I was playing a live Frank Sinatra album, *Live in Paris*, I forget what year. Hearing it made me want to leave immediately. It made me what to be out on the streets of New York, any city with life. Not like LA which is just death and memories.

1.2.96 1:56 p.m. Dublin Ireland I met up with Rick on the plane out of London to here. We hailed a taxi to the hotel and on the radio was Philomena Lynott telling stories about putting up Thin Lizzy when they would come off the road and how bad their van smelled of dirty clothes. The DJ asked her if she was going to be at the show and she said that of course she would. She said that she had a cold and had to rest so she said goodbye. It was so cool to get in the cab and immediately, the Lizzy trip had started.

When we checked into the hotel, we found out that some of the Lizzy people were going to be staying there as well. I met the original guitarist, Eric Bell, at check-in.

Rick and I went and walked around Grafton Street where all the stores are. Several people asked me why I was in town. 'For Phil, man!' The smile and the nod. It's early afternoon and the sun is out and the weather is very mild. It's like springtime. The streets are crowded. I wish I wasn't so tired but I will have to pass out for at least a few hours. No way am I going to make it all the way through to tonight.

1.3.96 1:24 a.m. Dublin Ireland Hung out with Scott Gorham for a couple of hours tonight. I was in my room and he called and said we should meet in the lobby. I went down there and he was waiting at the elevator. He looks pretty much the same as in pictures. Really cool guy as well. We sat in the lobby and talked for a long time. Rick came down as well. He told me and Rick some cool stories about Phil and touring with the band. It ends up that I will be singing 'Are You Ready?' with the band. He gave me a choice between either that or 'Suicide', which is a good song but not one of my favorites. 'Are You Ready?' is a good one to do. It was a blast hanging out with him. He said that Phil got in a lot of fights on the road. I never knew that about him. He said that it was hard on Phil growing up black in Ireland and he learned to fight early. He also said that Phil pushed everyone in the band hard to be better. Some of the stuff he told me I had read before in interviews but it was cool nonetheless to hang with the guy.

When Scott took off, Rick and I just looked at each other grinning. Rick is not given to being blown away by much but I could tell that he was. For myself, I was loving it. I live for stuff like this. Hanging with Scott Gorham and talking about one of the greatest bands ever. I don't think anyone I know gets so into this kind of thing this much. I guess I am a fan all the way.

Band practice is in the afternoon. That won't take long. I guess the next couple of days are going to be pretty easygoing. It will be strange not having to do something all the time.

1.4.96 10:03 a.m. Dublin Ireland Yesterday was fun. We got to The Point, the hall where the show is going to be. I watched Joe Elliott doing 'Suicide', 'Boys Are Back in Town' and 'Cowboy Song'. It was good. He can sing the songs ok and the band is totally tight. After a while I wandered around and ran into the Therapy? guys and met Joe Elliott who seems to be a very cool guy. A while after that it was time for me to sing with the band. I met John Sykes, a guitar player in one of the later lineups, Marco Mendoza, the bass player, and the drummer Brian Downey and Scott. We hit the song three times and it was great.

They got a big kick out of it and so did I. I don't know if they were used to someone hitting it that hard. After the first time through, they looked at me like I was nuts but they all started smiling and the next two times we were rockin'. What a kick in the ass that was.

After that I watched Therapy? play 'Bad Reputation' with the band and split back to the hotel. A few hours later Scott Gorham came down to my room and asked if I wanted to sing any other songs. I didn't because I didn't think I could do them justice. I was happy with just doing the one. I didn't want to let him down, but at the same time, I want to be good out there and not do anything less than rip it up.

We do it all again at soundcheck and then leave it until the show. This should be pretty great. I'm still amazed that I am getting to take part in this.

1.5.96 1:33 a.m. Dublin Ireland Did the show. What a blast that was. We tore it up. I wish I could have done the whole gig with them. It was over so fast. It was so cool to look out at the crowd who were going nuts and then look to my left and see Scott Gorham rocking out. It will stand as one of the high points of my life.

I met Philomena. She and I were sitting in the dressing room and she seemed really nervous. I introduced myself and she asked if I had a cigarette. I didn't but I went out and got her one. We spoke for a little while. She didn't know who I was. I figured she thought I was someone hanging out backstage. I didn't bother to tell her that I was going to play with the band.

All in all, it was a pretty strained event. The guys in the band were great and they played well, but in general, had an emptiness factor. I got out of there right before all the punters started leaving. I leave in a few hours to go to London. I'm ready for a new vibe.

1.6.96 10:28 a.m. London England Missed breakfast this morning. The only reason I stay at this place is because the breakfast is good and I missed it. My flight isn't for a long time and this is a bad thing because now I have to try to find edible food. Oh well, I guess I can eat in LA when I get there in about twenty hours.

Last night I had a speaking date here in London and it was a great time. The gig was at a place where I have done shows before, the Town and Country. It's now called the Forum. The inside of the place is kind of depressing. I could see steam coming out of my mouth when I was walking up to the dressing room. That's what I'll always associate with England and doing shows here – cold venues and poorly lit dressing rooms.

Walking up to the dressing room yesterday afternoon reminded me of the time I played with the Exploited at the Rainbow here in 1981. The place was freezing and the Exploited had taken what little food that was given to us out of our room and taken it up to theirs. We watched them walk out with it and the guy was so big we just stood there as he walked away grinning. Whenever I am anywhere in the British Isles, I am hungry or thinking about where I can be fed. I associate the whole place with hunger, cold, damp and dimly lit rooms. The people make up for any shortcomings, real or imagined. In Ireland people were so cool to me. I am sorry I didn't get a chance to get up to Scotland this time around. I always have a good time up there. Last night the audience was excellent.

It's easy to do a show with an audience that good. I have never had a lame audience for a spoken show here. In fact, quite the opposite. I hated leaving the stage last night. I could have gone on for another hour. I figure after two hours and forty-seven minutes, they can use a break from me and my big mouth. But that's always how I know I did a good one, when I start to miss them as I am walking off stage.

It's a strange relationship to have with people. I have had it for over fifteen years. I know so many strangers. I know that is a weird thing to say but it's true. These people I don't know but like very much somehow keep showing up and I keep feeling the need to give them everything I got when I'm up there. I read the mail and spend a lot of time thinking about them. I wonder what my life would be like without all these people interacting with me. At this point, it's all I know. I really don't much remember what I was like when I was twenty. It's been a strange way to get through the time. On the other hand, as far as knowing so many strangers, I guess that's the only kind of people I ever get to know.

Last night after I got back to the hotel, I started thinking about the whole Thin Lizzy experience that I just had. It made me feel sad and empty. It was great to do it and it was a blast meeting the guys and Philip's mother and all, but what I was onstage with two nights ago was not Thin Lizzy. It was an extremely good cover band doing the music of Thin Lizzy. As long as I can think of it that way, I am alright with it. It can't be Thin Lizzy without Phil. I guess that's what gets to me. The more people cheered and the more the guys laid into the music, which they did with energy and passion, the more Phil Lynott was painfully missing until the whole thing took on this air of desperation that made it impossible for me to stay to the end. I purposely got out of there before the band got off stage. I didn't want to see them or Philip's mother again that night, in that place, in that context. I think I would have started crying. I never knew Philip but I feel like I do in a way and when I play the band's music, I miss him. I know that sounds stupid but it's true. It's the same feeling I get when I listen to Hendrix. It's the friend that you never had that you know you'll always have. The fact that you didn't meet really doesn't matter. The whole venue was filled with people because a guy died. That was hard to deal with. You had to rock hard to keep from crying.

I remember when I was sitting alone in the dressing room with Philip's mother and for a moment we just stared at each other. She was elated that all these people were there to celebrate her son and at the same time she was nervous about it all. People treated her like royalty of course but I wondered what it would be like when she got home. Her ears ringing from the noise, the smell of beer and tobacco smoke in her clothes. A night she had been thinking about is now over. Her son is ten years gone and never coming back. The vast number of people that were at the show amplifies his absence, her loneliness. Her room is quiet. Time holds her in the past tense.

1.6.96 8:37 p.m. LA CA I got back here an hour ago. The flight was relatively painless at ten hours and twenty-two minutes. I was in a bad mood by the time we got to LA. It was a combination of having to listen to these two tourist couples talk very loudly about everything that is boring and that one of the men was working with his micro recorder and kept rewinding while the machine was in play. The sound made it impossible to think or read.

The book I was reading when he wasn't rewinding didn't help my mood either – the unauthorized biography of Frank Sinatra. I don't know how much of the book is true but it's an interesting read all the same. So many of the things that this book said he did, I would have done in the same situation. I love the parts about punching out the photographers and journalists. How righteous. So many of those people need a smack. Reading the book made me want tell the people across from me that I would have them killed if they didn't shut up, just like Frank. If you wrote a bad review about him, he would contact you and sometimes threaten you with a beating. People who got too close to him were worked over by his thugs. If any of this is true, he must be one bad motherfucker. The book said he fired people left and right and went ballistic on everyone all the time. I don't think I could ever be like that, but what a concept. It must have been a wild time being around him when Ava Gardner left him. One look at her and you know she was trouble on two legs.

I thought about Thin Lizzy a lot on the way back here. The whole thing makes me think that it's not always good to get all that close to what you want to see. Sometimes you can see too much. I wonder if I got a little closer than I should have on this one. It was an interesting experience but I don't know if it was the right thing to do. It was great to meet them and do the thing but it was a strange space to be in.

Travel sure is a strange thing. Several hours ago I was onstage in Dublin, Ireland. Now I'm back in my room with all this information. You always pay the price for experience. Sometimes you know it's going to hurt when you go in, but you go anyway.

SPAIN 1996

The airport was hot The airplane is completely packed, and hot. Behind me, student morons talk nonstop. The most useless noise polluting bullshit spews forth from their mouths in a relentless torrent.

'I've got "Walk Like an Egyptian" on my headphones!'

'Have we taken off yet?'

'You're stupid!'

How great would it be to take a length of pipe and randomly club some of these young travelers like seal pups while the rest of the economy section looked on in shocked and grateful disbelief.

I got up before the seat belt sign was turned off in an effort to use the toilet before any of the herd got the idea. I was two steps form the door when I was snaked by an old woman who shot past me. I turned and started back to my seat. I looked at the human sprawl that were looking at me like I was the in-flight entertainment. They looked like galley slaves – all those little eyeballs.

It would be great to see airplanes that were manually operated. Sets of pedals underneath each seat. Of course, only the economy section would be made to pedal, business and first class would be spared the endurance test. The flight attendants would double as the enforcers. 'Coffee, tea, or the lash?' It would give the students something to do with all that energy rather than blather on mindlessly. I wonder what they talk about over the rattle and hum of U2 records while they have sex. Do we really want to know? Do we really *need* to know the altitude we are climbing out of and the altitude we will be reaching for our trip? Hell no, but the pilot insists on telling us as well as filling us with more useless information. Another person on this flight who refuses to shut up.

The couple manacled next to me, a pair of seniors, are asleep for now. This is a six and half hour flight – New York to Madrid.

The idiots are up and working, trying to get around that beverage cart to the toilet. It seems like all of a sudden, the entire economy section has to go. They have no concept of space management. The carts have about two inches of clearance on either side. You know this because you have had your arm smashed and your foot ran over by the damn thing as it comes a' servin' down the aisle. The toilet seekers are not stopped by this, oh no. They stand stupidly, waiting for Beverage Cart Boy to figure something out. This usually entails the cart moving several seats down while a stranger stands on your feet and sticks an ass or crotch in your face and waits for the cart to pass. This is where the short blade palm knife would come in handy. Three to four violently administered puncture wounds to the buttocks will shift the priority of one of these food wasters quickly and efficiently.

All this negativity and I have not yet stated why I am trapped on this ship of fools in the first place. Rock and roll, man. We are playing a single festival date in Grenada, Spain. We arrive Friday, rock out Saturday and fly back to NYC on Monday. I do not know what other bands are on the bill or how many people are expected to show up. None of these facts matter to me. I'm just in it for the fury of the live experience. It doesn't matter where it is or whom it's with.

Things might actually be looking up. I located an unoccupied toilet. I noticed a thin slot over in the wall over the sink.

USED RAZOR BLADES

Over the writing is a drawing of an old two-sided shaving razor. I think that if I were to slash my wrists, I would be able to have the presence of mind to dispose of the blade properly. Hats off to anyone who could slip the razor through the slot while ceiling splattering arterial blood spray shot out of them. Another good thing is that the engine noise has turned the student backing track into a wordless hum.

The speaker over my head crackled,

'There has been a Bell-Atlantic pager misplaced. If anyone has found it, please make this known to a flight attendant.'

It's under my left foot and you're never seeing it again.

Several hours ago, I met David Lynch for lunch at his hotel. I had done a small part in his most recent film *Lost Highway*. It was an honor to work for him. What a brilliantly cool guy.

He had been in New York and New Jersey all week with Angelo Badalamente working on music for the film. I met him outside the elevator. His hair looked like a tornado. His eyes were wide and he was smiling.

'Hey man! Good deal!'

We went downstairs to eat. I could not help but ask him a lot of questions. When he was describing mixing music into a movie scene and how when it works, how amazing it is, the passion with which he described this and the intensity of his hand gestures were inspiring as hell. That and the smile that came with it was really amazing. It's so great to meet people who are older than you who have been doing what they love for longer than you have and finding out that they still love it with burning intensity. It makes me check myself. It's a good reference point. People like David are the real thing.

He is going be working on the film for several more months nonstop until it's finished.

We talked about Surrealism, media and music. I told him about hanging out at Sun Studios in Memphis a few weeks ago and how cool it was to stand in the same place where Jerry Lee Lewis recorded all his hits. David is way into music.

A couple of hours later: The inmates are asleep and one of those bland movies they always show on flights is playing. Wynona Ryder and a bunch of women sorting out their problems with men and their dicks. Chris, our guitar player, was so moved by the film that he walked over and told me he was going to have to hit me because the film bored him so much. He proceeded to hit me twice and staggered off into the darkness.

There's about three hours to go on this flight. The heat is on or the air conditioning is off, I don't know which.

I did an interview with a man yesterday. It was for an article about Black Flag. I didn't feel like being a part of this, but when I heard that the Ginn had participated in it, I figured I should at least have my say. I know that 'the Ginn' (that is the name which certain ex-constituents have crowned him with in honor of his perplexing, enigmatic propensities and paranoid demeanor) will never say anything good about me. The interviewer confirmed this.

I did not say anything untoward about the Ginn because he was, at one time, one of the most brilliant and unique musicians in America. He will always have my respect and gratitude. He will never know how many times that I and other band members had to defend him in front of disenchanted employees, bands on his label who felt betrayed and ripped off by him. With the truths I know about the Ginn, I could bury him in two hundred words or less, but why bother? I would rather just know what I know and let him live in his illusion and poor production values. I have infinitely bigger and more interesting fish to fry.

Still, spending an hour on the phone with the interviewer made me think of those days and all the tension that came with them. A lot of good music but not a lot of good times. It was never the lack of funds or organization that was hard to take. It was the distrust and knowing that you were always being watched and that you were just part of someone else's thing whose dimensions and expectations you would never be able to satisfy.

There are people you meet who are convinced that they don't need or deserve any happiness. I am one of them. I believe that happiness leads to complacency, weakness, boring output and excess body fat, and to a certain degree, I'm right. Happiness that dulls and numbs is one thing, but happiness that inspires one to create with fury and obsession is another thing altogether.

For myself, I have always liked the romance like that of the husband and wife in *The Addams Family*. I never saw the show more than a few times, but even at a young age, I was moved by the power with which her presence overwhelmed him. I know that's a pretty lame example but there's something there. It definitely explains my love of doo wop ballads, Thin Lizzy tearjerkers, and all those sad and beautiful songs that drive people out of rooms when

I play them over and over. The kind of songs I write all the time but never show to the band. I've always liked the romantic movies with the happy ending. I guess because I could leave the theater and not have to get any of it on me. I could go back to my solitary life which is the only one I have been able to understand. Not very brave I know, but I have spent countless hours thinking of how things could be as the miles screamed underneath the wheels. So many years of travel has made a daydreamer out of me. So many years spent *getting there*. Makes your mind wander out of the confines of the small enclosure you're forced to spend so much time in.

I have never spent much time finding out what life outside of touring was like – the life that most people have. Real life, I guess. On the other hand, life is real whether you're in Beverly Hills or on Death Row. Maybe the 'realness' is nothing more than the amount of hard times you encounter on your journey.

Perhaps I have lived in a bubble for the last decade and a half, but I doubt it. I could have gone for their reality and their bubble on many occasions when my conviction and will power flagged.

When people tell me I've sold out, I never wonder if they have sold out – just how many times and to what extent. I wonder how many times they really put their shit on the line and how many times they packed it in and went for the easier route that they said they would never take. You can say anything you want. We're all going to get it in the end. Am I rambling? Am I tired as hell and starting to hallucinate?

The students are starting to look funny to me as they line up to use the toilet. Their teacher, a woman I have dubbed 'The Woman Whose Mouth Will Not Close', is seated across from me and has been driving me insane for the last few hours just came up to me.

'May I ask you a question?'

I said no and kept on writing. After having to hear all the drivel that came out of her mouth relentlessly for over an hour, I figured that I was not in line to have to listen to this bore one nanosecond more than I already had.

Soon we will be in Spain. We played Madrid in 1994. Around soundcheck time, a kid on a bike got hit by a car right outside the venue. He was bleeding from his head but seemed to be ok.

We have another flight after we land in Madrid. It will be a long time before we get to the hotel. Today is a day off in a way. Been a while since I had one of those.

3.16.96 5:30 a.m. Grenada Spain Yesterday we landed in Madrid and had to hustle across that airport to catch the next plane to Malaga.

I was almost at my seat row having endured the phenomenon of waiting for people to find their seat, sit the fuck down and shut the fuck up. This time it was really bad. No one seemed to have any idea where they were supposed to sit. I stood watching people look at the ceiling and the seats for what seemed like an eternity. I was a few rows away from my seat when people started coming in from the rear of the aircraft towards the front. I could not help myself.

'What are you? Salmon swimming upstream to spawn? Why are you threatening the already tenuous relationship that we're having with efficiency here? Will you take your seats? Ladies and gentlemen, please! This is not a cattle car!'

The people who understood me thought I was funny. The rest thought I was a goddamn maniac.

Seats taken, we were soon on our way to Malaga. We arrived in no time. I was in a good mood because now we could go to the hotel and get some food. Due to my ignorance of the particulars of this trip, I didn't know that there was still a long van ride to our final destination of Grenada.

The countryside we passed made it worth the drive. Decaying buildings lined the road. Some without roofs had trees growing through them. Small, simple houses here and there. Lone farmers standing in the middle of fields.

Finally we got to Grenada, dumped the bags and ate. I found out that we had to go to the venue and do soundcheck in a couple of hours. So much for the day off.

I lay on my bed in my airless, tiny room having work-related dreams about missing the phone call to tell me to go to the lobby for the ride to soundcheck. I actually picked up the phone a couple of times after hearing it ring only to find out that it was the phone in the room next door.

A bit after ten that night we went to the venue to check out the rented gear and power it up. It was an outdoor venue. PA cabinets stood out in the rain and men onstage worked in the dark. The rental gear was up but there was no power to turn it on and see what it was like. It was cold as hell out there too. I thought about that, seeing we were going to be playing here in about twenty-three hours. It was easy to see that there was not going to be any soundcheck that night so we went back to the hotel.

I like it when we are all together. The stories start flying and the laughter increases. I like the acceptance that everyone seems to have for one another. These are very good people I work with. So many years and so many miles together. Something about time spent and distance traveled makes for a closeness that I have not known with anyone that I didn't do this with.

I can actually divide people into two camps: people I have been on the road with and people I haven't. They are two distinctly different relationships. Even the language used in conversation is different. There is an instant recognition with a fellow road animal. There is really nothing like it and I'm going to miss it when it's over.

It's not the same as it used to be. The old ways are no more. I distinctly remember coming back from one hundred and six shows all over the world with the band at the end of 1994 and feeling that I really hadn't been anywhere. The tour buses and hotels are good for getting some sleep for the gigs and enable us to play hard every night but we do not travel as low to the ground as we used to. As well, the places are so well traveled now. You end up on the bill with these baby bands that have not done anything more than one trite little record that has them on top of the world. Some of the thrill is gone. I watch these bands smirk through an uninspired set and think to myself, 'Do people really like this shit?' and then I hear the crowd roar when they get out there and I know it's true. That's what happened when I saw the Offspring play at a radio thing. This weak band playing this cute, pale imitation of fifteen year old music. I was repelled by the lameness and lack of substance while I watched the crowd lose their shit. I knew then that it was time to get out in a few years. If that's where music is going, then it's definitely time to split.

I still get off on the whole thing and would rather sleep at night than sit up with my head banging against a van window, but sometimes touring feels like a long tour of hotels and air conditioned rooms more than a trip down the road. There's no way it could stay the same though. It all changes. I'll get out before it gets too gross and the bands get too lightweight. I'm not going to stick around contemporary music for too long. Too safe, too many pretenders.

So now it's jet lag time in my airless little room. We play tonight.

3.18.96 1:07 a.m. Grenada Spain We went to the venue again in the morning to check out the gear and get a soundcheck. We got through a couple of songs before we were told there was no more time. They still didn't have their shit together and they're telling us that we don't have ours together. It started to remind me of almost every show we have ever done in Italy. A bunch of unprofessional posers acting like they know their job when all they really know how to do is eat and point at things. Of course we kept on playing and acting like they didn't exist, which to us, they didn't. Festival weasels. We were finally done and it sounded bad onstage like I figured it would. The ride back to the hotel was pure torture because the radio was on and this wretched song on Sting's new album played for almost the entire time we were in the van. Something about letting your soul be your guide. I can't believe he gets away with writing this crap and people eat it up. Oh I forgot, most people are mediocre and don't listen to the records they buy, don't taste the things they eat and don't care what poisonous crap they put into their bodies.

We were supposed to hit the stage at eleven. We left the hotel at ten for the venue which is ten minutes down the road. The festival was running late as expected. We eventually got onstage around two. It was really cold up there. I played in my usual two pairs of shorts and no shoes. My feet got so cold so quickly that I was stomping on cables and not even feeling it. First song in, I noticed that the monitors were feeding back badly. The entire stage was howling with low-end feedback. I knew immediately that it was going to be one of those bad concert experiences that crop up every once in a while.

I could not hear myself at all and within three songs, I had blown out my voice and had to croak for the rest of the gig. The songs were barely distinguishable from one to the next. The audience was in a bad mood as you would expect them to be as they had been outside in the cold since before noon.

We finished the gig past three and went back to the hotel.

I spent Sunday reading and sleeping. I wanted to be back in New York doing something constructive or on the way to the next gig. Sitting in the room was barely tolerable. The rest of the guys went to the Alhambra. I'm sure it was beautiful. I opted for solitude and some hours spent where I didn't have to talk on the phone and not be held to a deadline or appointment.

This faux bliss lasted a couple of hours at best. Soon I was stressing about not having things to do. I don't know what to do when my brain attacks me. I probably do not know myself all that well because I have filled my life with so much work and responsibility for others' projects. It's probably some off-the-rack psychosis. Instead of cleaning my own backyard, I only comment about the state of others. People see mine is overgrown and say, 'My, isn't he so good to give to others,' when maybe all it is, is some pathetic strain of cowardice.

Now it's early Monday morning and we leave for New York in a few hours. I wish I could have another crack at that gig. It sucks knowing that the thousands of people who watched us play had no idea of the audio hell we were in up there and how wretched the whole thing was – trying to give it all we had and knowing that it was not all we could have done. They will never know all the nights I spent on the bike working on my endurance just for this one show – that I had been working many nights getting myself ready for this and that I left feeling ripped off and unsatisfied.

3.19.96 3:16 a.m. NYC NY I got back here about twelve hours ago. The flight was packed. One of those massive planes with the huge center aisle. Next to me was the Vibrating Man. He jiggled both his legs so much that the entire section was moving with him. I knew that before the flight was over, I was going to have to kill him. Luckily he and his wife, after many trips to the smoking section from which they returned reeking, eventually moved over one seat that was vacated by a student.

I managed to fall asleep for a few hours and read for a few more and soon enough, the flight was over.

Now I'm up, jetlagging on the other side. The apartment is quiet, save for the heating pipes which are beating out a primitive clang every few minutes.

Band practice starts at one. No shows planned until we go to Poland in a couple of months.

Right now I'm thinking about the ride from Grenada to Malaga, watching the sun come up. Knowing that there are two flights with a four hour layover in the middle yet to go. So many mornings I have found myself in this position – heading 'home', whatever that means. It's times like this where I wonder if I have totally screwed up my life. Then I look at the tired faces around me and someone makes a joke and we're all laughing. It's then I come to the conclusion that there is no right thing except having the guts to go for what you want with the time you have here. And that's not a small task. It takes a lot of will power to go your own way. A lot of people think they are doing just that and they aren't. They are following in the footsteps of a not-so-hot-to-begin-with tradition. For this, life is not too short, but more horribly, very well suited. I'd rather do anything else.